Emerged Markets

For far too long, emerging markets and developing countries have played a subservient role in the global economy.

This book builds a compelling case that a new settlement is needed, that rebalances power, well beyond existing arrangements such as the G20, and creates a shared vision to build economic growth and prosperity. The alternative is a world which lurches from crisis to conflict, jeopardising peace and prosperity. The very phrase "emerging markets" connotes that some countries are still developing and cannot compete with mostly Western global economic heavyweights. But the rise of China and India has not been isolated phenomena, with many other emerged countries also becoming confident about their place in the world: these are emerged markets, not the Global South or the Third World. Although these emerged countries now dominate global trade and investment and are the biggest champions of globalisation, their dramatic increase in economic weight has not led to a commensurate increase in clout and influence on the world stage, due to fundamentally unchanged World War II-era structures and apparatus. Written by a global economics insider who has been in the room in multilateral, national, and private sector organisations, this book argues that the developed and emerged worlds should be positioned as equal economic partners, requiring dramatic adjustments in perceptions and power on the part of the developed world. Though clear-eyed about the ills that continue to exist in the emerged world, Vasuki Shastry explains why rich countries should be willing and open to learn from their success stories. He presents a reimagined narrative for the global economy, with more collaboration, less finger-pointing, and a confluence of equals in managing profound economic risks and opportunities, now and in the future.

Leaders in business, NGOs, and government, as well as students of business and international relations, will appreciate this thoughtful examination of what could happen if emerged and developed markets worked as equal partners for the common good.

Dr. Vasuki Shastry has spent much of his career working on and in emerged markets. He was a journalist in India, Singapore, and later in Indonesia, where he covered the Asian financial crisis and the fall of President Suharto in 1998. Pivoting from journalism, Shastry worked in communications and public affairs leadership roles at the International Monetary Fund in Washington D.C., Standard Chartered Bank in London, and the Monetary Authority of Singapore. Shastry serves on the advisory council of Chatham House (UK and the World program) and at the Institute of Human Rights and Business. He is the author of three previous books, writes a monthly column for *Forbes Asia,* and divides his time between Washington D.C. and Dubai.

"Vasuki Shastry, who has had a distinguished career at the IMF, charts the dizzying course of international relations from the end of the Cold War and America's brief unipolar moment, to the emerging multipolarity that characterises international relations in the twenty-first century. He analyses the decline of effective multilateralism and describes the inequality that disfigures a world in which great powers conduct international relations on the basis of might is right. He pleads instead for 'coexistent multilateralism', a world order in which the newly 'emerged' and status quo powers work cooperatively together, and warns of the perils, including the catastrophic impact of climate change and future pandemics, if they do not. His prescription may sound utopian in a period of renewed great power rivalry, but he paints a grim picture of the dystopian alternative."

– **Sir David Manning,** *Former U.K. Diplomat, Ambassador to the United States; Distinguished Fellow, Chatham House*

"Vasuki Shastry remains a keen observer of global economic trends. Following his provocative book questioning the prospects for an 'Asian Century', Shastry's latest oeuvre speculates on the implications of 'Emerging Economies' having 'Emerged'. Always thought-provoking, Shastry wields a fine pen."

– **Dr. Sanjaya Baru,** *Author, Editor, Media Advisor to Prime Minister Manmohan Singh*

Emerged Markets

The Global Economy's Better Half

Vasuki Shastry

Routledge
Taylor & Francis Group
NEW YORK AND LONDON

Designed cover image: Getty

First published 2026
by Routledge
605 Third Avenue, New York, NY 10158

and by Routledge
4 Park Square, Milton Park, Abingdon, Oxon, OX14 4RN

Routledge is an imprint of the Taylor & Francis Group, an informa business

ISBN: 9781032992983 (hbk)
ISBN: 9781032992976 (pbk)
ISBN: 9781003603375 (ebk)

DOI: 10.4324/9781003603375

Typeset in Sabon
by codeMantra

For Dion, and to Hyderabad, India, where it all began

"We are four large countries with abundant resources, large populations and diverse societies. We together account for almost one-fifth of the world's GDP. We aspire for rapid growth for ourselves and for an external environment that is conducive to our development goals. The people of our countries expect us to work together so as to bring the benefits of inclusive social and economic development to them"

Opening Statement by Indian Prime Minister Manmohan Singh, Second BRICS Summit, Brazil, April 15, 2010

"Inside the word 'Emergency' is 'Emerge', from an emergency, new things come forth. The old certainties are crumbling fast, but danger and possibilities are sisters"

Author Rebecca Solnit – Hope in the Dark:
The Untold History of People Power

Contents

Glossary

I have written this book with both the specialist and general reader in mind. Here is a helpful glossary of some of the technical phrases.

Capital flows The flow of private capital – through investment in stocks, bonds, direct investment, and other instruments – from both developed to developed nations and developed to emerged nations (and vice versa).

Creditor nations A group of wealthy nations traditionally led by America and Europe which provided much of the aid and financial assistance to poorer nations.

Deglobalisation Refers to a reduction in the level of integration in the global economy concerning the flow of goods, services, capital, and the flow of people.

Decoupling In the context of US-China trade and investment, this refers to the disengagement of both countries from each other's economies, which in practice is very difficult to achieve.

Economic statecraft Increasingly in usage and in practice, this refers to coercive economic tools and policies introduced by countries (targeting sanctions and other measures) aimed at achieving strategic geopolitical objectives.

Frontier economies Frontier economies like Nigeria are defined as such, representing a sub-set of emerging markets with less developed capital markets, economic frameworks, and liquidity.

Governance reforms This refers to how multilateral institutions – the United Nations, IMF, World Bank – are actually managed and led with a fair vote share and representation for emerged countries.

Middle powers This typically refers to large- or medium-sized nations (by population, economic wealth, geographic location, and other criteria) who are exercising greater power in world affairs. They remain less influential compared with a superpower like America.

Multi-alignment A foreign policy approach being pursued by middle powers like India and the UAE, in maintaining friendly ties with competing regional and global powers.

"Tall fence with a small yard" This phrase originated in a speech by former US National Security Advisor Jake Sullivan and describes America's efforts to limit access to advanced technology to rivals like China.

Also by the Author

Resurgent Indonesia – From Crisis to Confidence (2018)

Has Asia Lost It? Dynamic Past, Turbulent Future (2021)

The Notorious ESG: Business, Climate, and the Race to Save The Planet (2023)

Introduction

Emerging markets have truly emerged and are holding up the global economy.

Let me start with a strange question. What does the lead character in the 2019 Hollywood blockbuster *Once Upon a Time in Hollywood (OUATIH)* have to do with emerging markets, the topic of this book? It is all about perception and how it impacts the way the world looks at these markets.

Allow me to illustrate this further. In the movie, the lead character Rick Dalton (played by Leonardo di Caprio) is an actor facing career stagnation and relegated to playing the role of the heavy i.e. bad guy in a series of forgettable Westerns. Dalton meets with his agent Marv Schwarz, played by the incredible Al Pacino, to receive some sobering career advice. Schwarz bluntly tells him that his relegation as a heavy, where he gets punched by the good guys week after week, was an old trick by the studio to showcase younger lead characters and to destroy his own career prospects in the process. "You always play the bad guy in these shows", Schwarz asks, adding that over time his repeated punch ups will have a psychological effect on how the audience perceives Dalton, as a perennial loser and down goes his career as a leading man.

When I rewatched the movie recently, this scene resonated not least because I was in the throes of writing this book. Perception is everything. I have lived, breathed, and worked on emerging markets for much of my life – in India where I was born and started my career, and in Singapore, Indonesia, and more recently the UAE, with stops in Washington D.C. and London in between. My journalism career in Asia, followed by work for storied institutions – the IMF, Standard Chartered Bank, Singapore central bank – provided me with a valuable vantage point to witness the fall and rise of emerging markets since their humble origins in the 1980s. It has been an enormous privilege, witnessing first-hand the triumphs and tribulations of this vast swathe of humanity, home to over 6 billion people. At the same time, I have nursed the persistent suspicion that emerging

DOI: 10.4324/9781003603375-1

markets are not getting the respect and attention they deserve from peers in G7, advanced markets.

To put it bluntly, EMs have a Rick Dalton problem. They are regarded as a sidekick, even an afterthought sometimes, playing a marginal role to lead characters invariably drawn from the G7, who have positioned themselves unchallenged as superheroes at the vanguard of the global economy. Peak thinking of this kind surely happened in 1999, in the aftermath of the Asian financial crisis when *Time* magazine[1] placed the troika of Rubin, Summers, and Greenspan on the cover and boldly declared them to be "the committee to save the world". In this book, I argue that a reconstituted committee would include emerged rather than developed nations – perhaps including China, India, and Brazil, amongst others.

Although their role and influence have increased in recent decades, particularly with the dramatic rise of China and India, emerging markets are still regarded with barely concealed disdain in some sections of the advanced West. For example, look at global media coverage of EMs. They are regarded as the Wild East, home of crony capitalism, non-transparent business practices, and dramatically "different" from the more sophisticated West, which without irony is articulated to include less crony capitalism and more transparent business practices. Rhetorical note to self – did the global financial crisis originate in emerged or developed markets? Emerging market leaders also face challenges in getting a platform to highlight their thoughts and perspectives. A typical global economy panel at an international conference like Davos has a familiar list of speakers, drawn mainly from the US and Europe. A decade or so ago, there was a token Japanese on the panel, with the challenging task of speaking on behalf of Asia. In recent years, China's rise has made it impossible to ignore on such panels. Nevertheless, there are greater chances for a finance minister of a European country to feature on these panels compared with say someone from India or South Africa.

This book raises several challenges to the conventional storyline about supposedly backward emerging markets and rhetorically advanced developed markets. Before we get there, we must focus on labels. The label emerging market is no longer a fit-for-purpose description to describe the fast growing, vibrant, and dynamic segment of the global economy. I argue that these markets have emerged, they represent the global economy's better half, and they deserve to be defined as emerged markets, rather than merely emerging markets. The nomenclature is important because as Rick Dalton discovers in *OUATIH,* his career trajectory changes dramatically when he pivots from side roles to that of a leading man. Emerged markets, in my view, are the leading men and women of today's global economy. To be sure, the rich world has not faded into insignificance, but they should learn to share screen space and narratives with the new stars on the block.

If the sheer economic weight of the global economy is factored in, it is the rich nations who risk being relegated to the role of a sidekick. Last year, the combined economies of the original BRICS economies – China, India, Brazil, South Africa, Russia – were more than half of the size of the combined G7 in nominal dollar terms and some $10 trillion *larger* when calculated at purchasing power parity. S & P Global projects[2] that EMs will play a crucial role in shaping the global economy, contributing about 65% of global economic growth, with nine key emerging markets ranking amongst the 20 largest economies.

These markets, one, are also trade superpowers. China alone recorded overall trade i.e. exports and imports of $6.1 trillion in 2024 and registered a phenomenal trade surplus of just under $1 trillion, about the same level of annual trade it does with ASEAN. It is not surprising that China's surplus has created considerable angst in countries and regions which are in deep deficit with the country. Besides America (trade deficit of $300 billion), China has also a disproportionately advantageous trade relationship with Asean (surplus of $200 billion) and the European Union (surplus of around $330 billion). To be sure, other Asian countries have also notched up considerable trade surpluses with America, its major trading partner. Vietnam enjoys a surplus of around $120 billion, triggering a wave of tariffs from the second Trump administration targeting Hanoi but also literally every country on earth which trades with America.

This unprecedented level of surpluses (and deficits) has created shock and awe in the global trading system and essentially led to its current standstill situation, where major trading nations no longer trust multilateral forums like the World Trade Organisation (WTO) to function effectively and deliver on its mandate. As Director General Ngozi Okonjo-Iweala warned in the organisation's 2025 annual report[3] that since its creation, open and predictable international markets anchored in WTO rules and norms have made a significant contribution to strengthening the global economy.

> Nevertheless, the global trading system is today experiencing its worst disruptions since the Second World War. Multilateral cooperation itself is being called into question...One silver lining of the current disruptions is that they have reminded many governments, businesses, and households why the predictable trading conditions they had come to take for granted are so valuable.

Try making the same case with the second Trump administration and you are likely to fall short. Here is US Trade Representative Jamieson Greer[4] on the system's flaws. "Our current, nameless global order, which is dominated by the World Trade Organisation and is notionally designed to pursue economic efficiency and regulate the trade policies of its 166 member countries, is untenable and unsustainable". In his view, the US has "paid for the system" with the loss of industrial jobs and economic security, other countries have been unable to make needed reforms, and the biggest winner has been China, with its state-owned enterprises and five-year plans. Taking a deep breath, I can pronounce that the WTO-led global trading system is either in deep peril or worse in the process of getting dismantled. It will have costs, explicit and implicit, on the future of the global economy as countries and economic blocs pull away from the multilateral order and embark on bilateral and regional trading arrangements, which is increasingly becoming the norm.

Which brings me to the scope of the book. This may well turn into a book on the future of trade alone and I resisted the temptation of going in that direction. Yes, trade dislocation will have profound economic and social consequences all over the world and deserves a tome of its own. I do hear the commentary that the rest of the world will do just as well without American participation in the trading order. To that chestnut, my response would be it is wishful thinking to believe that any country or region can replace the might of the American consumer and his or her appetite to buy, buy, and buy. Even the surge in intra-regional trade, between China and Asean, for example, can be explained by supply chain movements of components destined for China for final assembly and export to America. In the absence of American participation and benevolence, the global trading order is going to change dramatically in the next few years with uncertain prospects. By the time you read this, America may well have either decided to remain within the existing system or reconfigured it entirely to suit its needs.

Which is why as I embarked on the book project, I decided to leave trade aside and focus on the other pillars of globalisation – the free movement of capital, and of people, to provide a nuanced account of how the emerged world is exerting greater control over world affairs. This a secular rather than a cyclical trend and here to stay. What exactly do I mean by the emerged world? It is certainly not the lumpy and patronising "Global South" label currently applied to much of the developing world. In my definition, the group of countries can be sliced and diced in different ways. The Morgan Stanley MSCI Emerging Markets Index, for example, includes Brazil, Chile, China, Colombia, the Czech Republic, Egypt, Greece, Hungary, India, Indonesia, Korea, Kuwait, Malaysia, Mexico, Peru, the Philippines, Poland, Saudi Arabia, South Africa, Taiwan, Thailand, Turkey, and the UAE. There is some overlap here with the expanded BRICS grouping, which currently comprises 11 members which includes Ethiopia and Iran. In addition, the G20 grouping includes the original BRICS plus Argentina. For the sake of simplicity, my definition of the emerged world excludes the likes of the Czech Republic, Greece, and Hungary (mainly because they are members of the European Union) and includes the MSCI, G20, and BRICS membership, along with the GCC and Asean groupings. This, in my book, is the emerged world. I also recognise that this leaves out a great number of low-income countries across the world (in Africa, the South Pacific, Latin America, and the Caribbean), who hopefully will benefit from the rising tide of the emerged world. The combined GDP of the BRICS and ASEAN grouping is currently around $34 trillion, accounting for a third of global GDP (around $110 trillion) and smaller of course than the combined G7 GDP of around $56 trillion. The interesting aspect of these numbers are how fast the emerged world is catching up. In 2000, the combined G7 GDP was around $26 trillion, whilst the BRICS and Asean share was in the low single digits.

Allow me to bring in the quibblers and the naysayers to make their case that my overall thesis is built on weak foundations. The first objection is from the market gurus, who proclaim that emerging markets, as an asset class, have consistently underperformed advanced markets like America and therefore deserve the emerging label. "The last time emerging markets were doing this badly the term "emerging markets" hadn't been coined yet" *The Wall Street Journal* declared in November 2024 "That spells opportunity, and the greatest spoils might go to those investors who are the boldest and also willing to look past that poorly defined category". I delve into the history of emerging markets in the next chapter but would like to push back on the proposition that dollar-based market returns should be *the* criteria to permanently relegate EMs into the second or third rung of the global economy. By this market return criteria, Europe would also qualify for relegation because its market performance over the past decade vis-à-vis America's S & P 500 has been abysmal. Since 2015, the S & P Global, led by the outperformance of America's Big Tech majors, has generated cumulative gains three times higher than those of European stocks. In the emerged world, India has also been a stand-out performer, delivering an impressive 18% annualised return in dollar terms since 2020, compared with a lower 4% generated by the overall asset class in the same period.

So, let's agree to set aside market returns and expectations of the investor class as the only criteria to judge if emerged markets deserve greater respect and attention on resolving global economic and security challenges. The quibblers are also likely to point out that although growth in emerged markets is real, these countries will never quite catch up to the living standards of the advanced west and Japan. This is a point made by S & P Global as well, and I acknowledge that if the contest is about measuring per capita GDP rather than absolute GDP, the race is titled in favour of nations which are currently rich and glorious. Besides America, Canada, Australia, New Zealand, and Europe, this exclusive club includes oil-rich nations in the Gulf, Japan, and the four Asian tigers. China (estimated 2025 GDP

$16 trillion, per capita GDP of around $13,000) is still not an economic match to its principal rival, America (GDP of $30 trillion and per capita GDP of $89,000). This principle – of the rich lording over the poor – is a uniquely 19th- and 20th-century construct, which created the conditions for colonialism and other excesses. I submit that the current challenges faced by the global economy and indeed of planet Earth requires a new framing built on the principles of equality, capacity, and a shared vision to promote sustained economic growth, peace, and stability. Or as the World Bank's renewed mission statement puts it, the goal is to end extreme poverty and boost shared prosperity on a liveable planet.

Equality or providing equal terms for the entire international community is a difficult concept to digest for powerful nations. In the last chapter, I discuss principles of fairness and justice in global affairs, but it is useful to dwell on the principle of equality and equity. The preamble of the United Nations (UN) charter, agreed at the end of World War II, admirably sets out high purpose goals, which I quote below in full:

> We the People of the United Nations Determined to save succeeding generations from the scrouge of war, which twice in our lifetime has brought untold sorrow to mankind, and to reaffirm faith in fundamental human rights, in the dignity and worth of the human person, in the equal rights of men and women and of nations large and small, and to establish conditions under which justice and respect for the obligations arising from the treaties and other sources of international law can be maintained, and to promote social progress and better standards of life in larger freedom.

Cynical readers will be right when they point out that large sections of the UN Charter have been followed in the breach. There are conflict zones all over the world – the Middle East, many parts of Africa, Russia/Ukraine, India-Pakistan to name a few – without an easy resolution. The Security Council, with its five permanent members granted with extraordinary veto power, is a relic of the post-World War II era, and any significant chances of reform are blocked by status quo powers, which includes emerged China. Arguably, the world of 1950, with a small, exclusive group of rich nations separated by a vast developing world required a different approach to global governance. Many developed nations in Europe were emerging from the horrors of the war and their efforts were supported by initiatives like the Marshall Plan. Simultaneously, the developing world was emerging from centuries of European colonialism with a spectacular jump in the number of newly independent nations in the 1950s and 1960s.

While I don't want to dwell on the impact of colonialism in undermining the economic and social capacity of the ruled, which has been documented elsewhere, the newly independent nations did not shirk from their responsibility in commenting on and intervening on important global issues. The decade of the 1950s saw the birth of the non-aligned movement (NAM), led by India, China, Egypt, Indonesia, and Yugoslavia, in pushing back against Western interference in countries as diverse as Congo, Vietnam, and Latin America. While the NAM movement sputtered in the following decades for complicated reasons,[5] echoes of its ideals are manifestly present in today's BRICS grouping and other initiatives aimed at strengthening the voice and representation of developing nations in the world order.

The crux of the matter is that the NAM grouping of the 1950s and 1960s lacked the financial resources and the capacity to effectively intervene in world affairs. My country of birth, India, faced food shortages and a famine in the 1960s and depended on American food donations. A similar saga unfolded in Africa, where nations faced civil strife, coups, and economic shocks. By design, the rules of the international game and much of the power were skewed heavily in favour of wealthy nations. *By the most objective yardsticks, this is simply not the case today.* The emerged world has demonstrated that it possesses the commitment and the capacity to effectively manage or even mismanage world affairs (look at Chapter 2), just as their rich peers have done. China's Belt Road Initiative, which I excoriate in a subsequent chapter for mismanagement, nevertheless demonstrates that the category of nations providing aid, and those receiving it, has been upended. During Sri Lanka's mini-revolution of 2022 and the economic crisis which preceded it, India stepped in along with the IMF to provide substantial financial assistance. During the devastating Indian Ocean tsunami of 2004, tiny Singapore shocked its neighbours with the capabilities of its armed forces in delivering aid and in clearing entire cities of rubble caused by the earthquake.

> The Singapore Armed Forces also provided infrastructural support such as a mobile air traffic tower to ease traffic congestion in Banda Aceh, a portable water purification plant, telecommunications equipment to improve the communications network, and a modular building which served as a coordination centre for relief operations, says an official Singapore government report[6] on tsunami assistance, a far cry from the period when disaster assistance primarily originated from the rich world.

Equally significant is the flow of ideas and capital, which I discuss in two separate chapters, where the emerged world is not only learning from each other, but investment flows are also headed east to east. Who would have imagined, for example, that the UAE would become Africa's largest foreign investor, with $44 billion committed in 2024, nearly matching the combined investments of the UK and China.[7] Ironically enough the emerged world – China, India, Singapore, Brazil, Taiwan, Saudi Arabia, the UAE, and others – is also amongst the world's largest holders of US Treasuries, bolstering the dollar's reserve currency status.

To use a much-abused phrase in economics, this is the new normal i.e. the evident abilities of the emerged world in extending help, ideas, capital to other nations in need, which is no longer matched by the G7 or multilateral agencies because of their dwindling generosity. This reality is unfortunately not matched with a commensurate increase in the power and influence of the emerged world. The G20 was a dramatically positive step in global governance but it has stagnated in recent years. It is not just the financial capacity of the emerged world which has dramatically changed since the low-growth era of the 1950s and 1960s. In cutting edge areas like electric vehicles, solar, digital identity, and even in oil refining, the emerged world is showing the way by originating innovation which has widespread relevance and application in both the developed and developing worlds. I highlight a few of these as case studies in the book with the caveat that these are not the only examples of emerged world expansion and innovation. I could have picked Brazil's *Bolsa Familia* as a model social welfare program that provides conditional cash transfers to the poor, which has wide applications in the developing world. Kenya's MPesa mobile money transfer and savings platform democratised finance in sub-Saharan Africa, just as Bangladeshi innovation in microfinance achieved several decades earlier. Morocco has also positioned itself as a major automobile manufacturer for Europe and its banks have a growing footprint presence in Africa. Important lesson here is that when you drop your biases and dig deep enough, the emerged world will reveal itself to be as innovative as its rich counterparts.

The emerged world is confident about its own abilities, and this is another compelling reason why it should be on the high table of global governance – the world is fracturing, the rich world has turned its back on globalisation, and systemic threats for the planet from pandemics and climate change are proliferating. The rich world's reversal on globalisation is not necessarily a Trump phenomenon, as citizens of rich nations have been sceptical about its merits for a decade or so before his political rise. However, the way the second Trump administration is treating its allies and partners, backed by policy actions, signifies that America no longer believes in the multilateral system it created. Singapore's former Foreign Minister George Yeo put it best recently, "Well, Trump is going back to an old world where there is no WTO, no MFN,[8] where trade is part of politics, part of relationships"; he told China's CGTN recently, "I like you, I need you more, so we have one regime. I don't like you; you need me more; we have another regime".

The Trump administration's economic actions since 2025 enjoys support from a broad segment of the electorate, who have turned deeply sceptical about the merits of globalisation. In November 2023, American Compass partnered with polling firm YouGov to survey[9] 1,000 Americans about their views of globalisation. The survey found that by a 41–28% margin, Americans said they have "personally benefitted rather than suffered" from America's embrace of globalisation. Yet at the same time, by a 47–33% margin, they said that the nation has suffered rather than benefited. "The general view that globalisation has harmed the nation is consistent with strong beliefs that both manufacturing and place matter – two judgments at odds with the pro-globalisation consensus among economists", their survey concludes.

In 2016, the year Trump was elected to his first term in America, polling firm YouGov polled[10] 20,000 people in 19 countries to ascertain their attitudes towards globalisation.

> Unsurprisingly, the countries that are the biggest enthusiasts of globalisation are the ones that have benefitted most from it – the poorer nations of East and South East Asia. Here, belief that globalisation is a force for good reaches at least 70% in all countries, and as high as 91% in Vietnam.

It is countries like Vietnam and its neighbours in the region which are deeply aggrieved and impacted since the public mood in America has shifted and the second Trump administration erects higher tariff barriers on imports. In the peak globalisation era, Vietnam regarded itself as being uniquely positioned to benefit from trade and investment tailwinds, which catapulted the country from a dirt-poor low-income country in the 1980s into a confident middle-income one at the turn of the 2020s. However, the country is facing considerable headwinds as it faces a penalty for exporting large quantities of goods to America, its most important trading partner.

Vietnam's challenges are mirrored in much of the emerged world and economists have come up with several apt labels to describe this malady – geoeconomic fragmentation, decoupling, deglobalisation. They all mean different things of course (see glossary) with some similarities. While tangible evidence about fragmentation or deglobalisation is hard to come by, the consensus in the policy community is that these phenomena are perhaps inevitable. "The global economy may be on the brink of a reversal of the steady increase in integration that characterised the second half of the 20th century", the IMF cautioned[11] in January 2023 "The increasing scepticism toward multilateralism contributed to the growing appeal of inward-looking policies, with policymakers becoming more receptive to erecting barriers between nations, including in the areas of trade, capital, migration, and technology sharing". The emerged world, which stands to lose the most if these economic phenomena gain momentum, has a shared interest in advocating for and defending the principles of open markets and multilateralism. This, in effect, is the principal theme of the book.

This is a good opportunity for me to emphasise what the book is *not* about. It is not primarily about trade as highlighted earlier. First and foremost, this is not a book which unconditionally pushes the point about the superiority of the emerged world vis-à-vis rich countries. There are many other books which have taken this approach. I don't gloss over the pressing problems faced by the emerged world – poverty, inequality, environmental devastation, to name a few. However, I believe that these problems can be resolved under more equitable terms with the support and cooperation of rich nations and the multilateral system. Second, this is not a book *only* about superpower contestation between the US and China. While I unavoidably focus on the US-China competition in several chapters, the objective of the book is to provide a perspective on the rest of the emerged world. There are also too many books on the market which take an ideological view about American or Chinese exceptionalism, and I wanted to pursue a different storyline. Finally, this is not a book about the merits of competing political systems i.e. the perceived superiority of democracy over authoritarianism or vice versa. I am not a political ideologue, but I do have strong personal views on this topic. But the profound global problems we are facing today cannot be simply resolved by expressing a preference to any political system, particularly as democratic systems themselves in the west are developing authoritarian characteristics. Like it or not, this is the age of the strongman in the developed and emerged worlds. Take your pick from Trump, Orban, Putin, Erdogan, Xi, and Modi.

A word about how the book is structured. Section I is titled "The Pivot" as it focuses on five aspects of the rise of the emerged world, starting with history and followed by power, capital, platforms, and ideas. Section II, "The Case Studies" is devoted to China's rise as an EV powerhouse, India's pathbreaking digital identity program, and the improbable commissioning of one of the world's largest oil refineries in Nigeria. Section III, "The Fault Lines", focuses on the youth bulge in the emerged world and the concluding chapter has wishful thinking (as some might argue) as to why coexistence should be the governing principle for a world in turmoil. A quick word about methodology. I researched the book the old-fashioned way and did not use AI tools, which are pervasive. I spoke to several people in the developed and emerged worlds to interrogate the themes showcased in the book, many of whom I name in the acknowledgements. Propitiously for me, much of the research happened quite organically in my roles as researcher, advisor, consultant, and my prior work in the emerged world. There also are bound to be real or potential conflicts of interest between these worlds and the book itself, and I have disclosed them upfront.

Finally, this book is targeted both at the specialist audience and the general reader. I have attempted to simplify complex economic and geopolitical concepts and have used examples from popular Hollywood culture (of which I am an unashamed fan) to illustrate the point better. The emerged world of course also excels in popular culture (Korea, Bollywood, Tollywood, to name a few) but let's all agree that Hollywood still has the global reach.

I hope you enjoy the book, starting with a history of emerging markets, where I have the privilege of introducing my younger self.

Notes

1 Time magazine, February 15, 1999. Robert Rubin was Treasury Secretary, Larry Summers his deputy, and Alan Greenspan the Chairman of the Federal Reserve.
2 Emerging Markets – A Decisive Decade, S & P Global, October 18, 2024. The nine key markets referenced include China, India, Brazil, South Korea, Indonesia, Saudi Arabia, Poland, Mexico, and Turkiye.
3 World Trade Organisation, 2025 Annual Report.
4 Why we remade the global order – oped contribution by US Trade Representative Jamieson Greer, August 7, 2025.
5 The NAM movement eventually proved to be unwieldy with members pursuing contradictory and conflicting goals. The movement also operated during the Cold War in the shadow of great power rivalry, which impacted the grouping's ability to act cohesively.
6 "Operation Flying Eagle" is activated after Asian tsunami – archived article in the National Library Board, Singapore.
7 Data from Semafor Africa, August 1, 2025.
8 MFN stands for most favoured nation, a trading status bestowed by nations to each other granting privileged access to their respective markets.
9 The American Rejection of Globalisation – American Compass-YouGov survey, January 2024.
10 YouGov international survey on globalisation – November 2016.
11 Geoeconomic fragmentation and the future of multilateralism – IMF, January 2023.

Section I

The Pivot

Chapter 1

History

A long time ago, in emerging markets far, far away

Nothing succeeds like excess.

Any historical account of emerging markets starts with debt raising, lots of it, and ends in default and crisis, predictably. So went the conventional wisdom throughout the 1990s, a momentous period where I had an incredible ringside seat.

Let's start at the beginning, Bombay, India, circa 1988. I was a young, relatively inexperienced business journalist unwittingly thrown into the deep end of international finance. The inciting incident was the launch of two offshore India Funds – in New York (1988) and London (1986) – by the Unit Trust of India (UTI), a state-owned mutual fund which had a near monopoly over the country's asset management industry. What made this launch unique at the time was the issuer, in effect the Indian government, which had been shut for foreign investment for several decades and was gingerly testing global financial waters for the very first time. Also unique for the New York offering was the involvement of blue-blooded investment banks, Merrill Lynch and Nomura, for shepherding the transaction to international investors. While the Indian economy was resolutely shut to outsiders, it must be said that the country was not like the former Soviet Union or North Korea. Foreign banks and bankers retained a presence in the country but deal size and fees, the *raison d'etre* of investment banking, were leaner compared with Asian peers. But India was regarded as the market of the future, very much like China, which had opened nearly a decade earlier.

Therefore, it was a sight to behold as well-heeled investment bankers descended on Bombay – from Hong Kong, London, and New York – to prepare for the launch and to embark on a series of road shows all over the world. Ground Zero for launch preparations was The Oberoi hotel, one of two luxury hotels in south Bombay. I am still in touch with a few of those international bankers, greying in the temples as I do, and they

DOI: 10.4324/9781003603375-3

get breathless recalling that momentous foray by India. Never mind that things did not go as well as planned.

Some context setting is important here. India was a minnow in the global economy at the time, with a modest GDP ($320 billion) and an anaemic growth trajectory going all the way back to the 1950s (of around 3% annually), which was memorably described by economist Raj Krishna as constituting the "Hindu rate of growth". India's share of global GDP had also shrunk from its glory days of the 19th century, when China and India together accounted for over half of global output, to an abysmal 3%. In terms of global economic power, India had very little of it (per capita GDP was in three digits – $360) and the country was an aid recipient. Since 1958, the World Bank organised the Aid India Consortium which brought together donor nations and multilateral agencies in an annual dialogue with the government to determine the level of aid the country would receive. Looking back, it must have been a humiliating experience for a proud, independent nation to petition Western nations for support, including food aid when supplies ran perilously low in the mid-1960s.

At the same time, it must be said that there was a great deal of self-inflicted policy errors on the part of successive governments, who pursued an ill-advised economic path centred on self-reliance and placed the state at the commanding heights of the economy. A senior Indian diplomat wistfully told me in 1989 that the two countries which had essentially created capitalism – India, through the medieval *hundi* system, the earliest variant of a credit instrument, and China, through the export-driven commodity model (mainly tea) in the 16th through 18th century – had forgotten the lessons and embraced economic statism instead.

While the ticket size of the India Growth Fund (IGF), listed in New York, was a relatively modest $100 million, the bankers told me that the Merrill Lynch CEO at the time (the late Jerome P. Kenney) had stayed up all night to check the prospectus. Such was the momentous nature of the launch. As it happens, the launch of the IGF was a canary in the coalmine event for the Indian economy and I don't mean this in a positive way. This is because less than three years later, India plunged into a balance of payments crisis which required a bailout from the International Monetary Fund (IMF) and serious soul-searching ensued amongst policymakers about the perilous nature of the country's economic mismanagement and premature dalliance with global finance.

The New York listing of the IGF also became a hostage to external economic developments, which continue to frustrate and bedevil policymakers in emerging markets. Let's turn to my younger self[1] for insights on what happened with the launch of the IGF. The mood music going into the launch was extremely favourable, I wrote. "The Indian economy was shaping up well despite last year's terrible drought, industrial output was looking up, and corporate performance was highly encouraging. What's more, after 18-months of uncertainty the stock markets were staging a smart rally". In the period running up to the August 1988 launch, the investor response was overwhelming, informal commitments totalled $126 million, a significant over-subscription.

> However, these commitments evaporated as the opening day approached and UTI had to take the extreme measure of scaling down its size, from $100 million to $60 million. The India Growth Fund was fully subscribed but not before having raised a lot of controversy.

What went wrong? In a word, the Federal Reserve Board announced an increase in interest rates that August, unnerving sentiment and forced potential IGF investors to reallocate money towards safer haven dollar assets. Merrill Lynch and Nomura had no choice in recommending a significant cut in the IGF offer size.

This was not the first or even the last time that an emerging market country has been held hostage to distant monetary policy developments in America or Europe. As emerging markets become more integrated into the global economy and indeed have become drivers of global growth, as we will unpack in following chapters, it is still amazing to see them penalised for repeated policy errors by the Federal Reserve – witness the market jitters after the May 2013 "taper tantrum",[2] or the post-pandemic failure to anticipate a sharp increase in inflation as shining examples. Commenting on the taper tantrum and its invidious impact on emerging market policies, former Indian central bank governor Raghuram Rajan had a simple message[3] to rich country central bankers during his tenure – let's coordinate our policies better. "I suggest that, at the very least, central banks reinterpret their domestic mandate to take into account other country reactions over time (and not just the immediate feedback effects), and thus become more sensitive to spillovers". Spillovers being "economicese" for the impact, intended and unintended, that one large country's economic policies have across the world. Today, it is regarded as acceptable for the rest of the world to absorb massive policy shocks originating in the west, despite them being innocent bystanders in many cases.

Now, many readers are bound to object to my characterisation of emerging markets being hostages to economic fortune. They will rightly point out that many of these countries, with China and India being the most spectacular examples, have pursued policies to benefit from the rise of globalisation. The argument goes that by opening their markets for trade and investment, countries were able to accelerate growth, reduce poverty, and increase economic opportunity. At the same time, they must be prepared to play by the rules of global finance set by the west, where emerging markets expose themselves to capitalist market forces which could either enrich or pauperise them, the latter being the norm during a dramatic upsurge in emerging market financial crises during the 1990s, which we will get to shortly.

Some historical context is important before we explore the nature, impact, and international response to the EM crisis episodes during that period. Some basic facts first. What exactly are emerging markets, who defined them as such, and why was there a need to establish a new financial asset category? Credit for coining the phrase, by popular acclaim, goes to Antoine van Agtmael, an economist at the World Bank's private sector arm International Finance Corporation (IFC). Van Agtmael came up with the emerging markets label while designing an equity investment fund targeting developing countries. The popular and in my view demeaning phraseology at the time was the third world, which implied that a vast mass of humanity was living in a parallel, less developed, and less deserving universe.

> The term "emerging markets" is created by IFC staff member Antoine van Agtmael while promoting a global listed equity investment fund for developing countries. The term will change the financial world's perception of developing countries and define a new asset class,

the IFC announced on January 1, 1981. The launch of the IFC-supported fund paved the way for developing countries to access international capital markets, as India did only seven years later.

The world as we know it today was a very different place in 1981. China had just opened two years earlier while vast swathes of the developing world, India included, were firmly shut to free trade and investment. There was one remarkable exception of course in East Asia, where Japan and the Asian tigers (Korea, Taiwan, Hong Kong, and Singapore) had pursued exceptional economic and social policies to achieve developed country status in three short decades, a record not emulated since anywhere in the world. By 1990 when I moved to Singapore, the city-state was the epitome of the first world with strong social and physical infrastructure, well-developed financial markets, and a government desperately keen to invest in skills to ensure that the country remained at the cutting edge. It was the success of Japan and the Asian tigers which motivated the three Asian laggards – China, Vietnam, and India – to pursue copybook economic policies in the 1980s to catch up with their richer Asian peers.

Things in financial markets have also never been the same since 1981, when IFC created the new EM asset class. As early as 1993, Federal Reserve Bank of New York economist John Mullin was celebrating[4] the rise of EMs as an asset class. Between 1976 and 1982, he estimated that annualised equity returns exceeded 20% in Argentina, Chile, Mexico, South Korea, and Thailand. Equity returns in Chile and Mexico soared to almost 50%

during 1990–1992. Mullin's analysis showed that across national markets, equity returns had borne a positive relationship to measures of economic performance, such as rates of export growth and dividend-per-share growth.

> Nevertheless, the extraordinary equity returns registered by several developing country markets in recent years have exceeded levels that can be explained by measures to ex ante risk and ex post macroeconomic performance. Returns in these countries appear to reflect fundamental structural changes that have increased investor demand for developing country-equity shares.

All this optimism would evaporate soon, and investors headed to the exits as we will discover shortly, starting with the prolonged and brutal debt crisis in Latin America.

Even factoring in the crisis of the 1980s and 1990s, EMs as an asset class have matured since their 1981 birth. Morgan Stanley estimates[5] that the emerging market share of global market capitalisation (which is the total value of stocks listed all over the world, developed and developing) was around 26% in 2021 (which has held since), a significant advance from 19% in 2009. This share, however, was still lower than the EM share of global GDP during that year, which was an impressive 39%.

> Over time we expect the EM global market cap share to rise and potentially converge with its GDP share, as rising incomes give more and more people the means to invest in stocks through retirement funds, insurance policies, and other increasingly sophisticated financial products.

Now that we have established the current performance and early promise of EMs as an asset class, it is useful to go back in time to examine what went wrong in the 1990s, an unstable period characterised by an epidemic of economic and financial crisis. In retrospect, the root cause of the crisis had a lot to do with a country's decision to opening up to global markets, because there was a huge mismatch in the sequencing and calibration of economic reforms, which eventually upended the economic, political, and social fortunes of countries as diverse as India, Mexico, and Indonesia, the three countries I am most familiar with. There was an equally significant (and arguably more turbulent) reform experience in Russia and Eastern European countries, emerging from the collapse of the Soviet Union.

A common theme from these episodes reveals two shortcomings on the part of the rich countries and the multilateral system they supported. First, despite the best of intentions, the quality of advice they offered was inconsistent, driven in many cases by ideology (one example being the repeated mantra that capitalism was superior to communism or socialism) rather than the specific circumstances faced by the country. Second, even the rich world has learnt this lesson the hard way. Nobody can control the beast that has become financial markets, demonstrated by Clinton advisor James Carville declaring in 1992 that he wished to be reincarnated as the bond market, so awestruck he was with its powers over political and economic outcomes. The ideological element of advice being proffered to emerging markets fell under an umbrella or platform conveniently labelled as the Washington Consensus (hereinafter referred to as the Consensus, because I don't wish to insult the originators with the WC label!). What or who was the Washington Consensus? Let's not beat around the bush and go directly to the source, the late, great economist John Williamson who coined the phrase in 1989. Speaking at the World Bank in 2004,[6] Williamson explained the origins of the phrase and why he felt it was important policy advice, with an initial focus on Latin American nations emerging from the debt crisis.

> The Washington Consensus as I originally formulated it was not written as a policy prescription for development: it was a list of policies that I claimed were widely desirable in Latin America as of the date the list was compiled, namely the second half of 1989.

What exactly were the list of policies which Williamson had in mind? The ten policies which he articulated on include:

- Reduce national budget deficits – Self-explanatory as high budget deficits impede government spending on critical areas like health, education.
- Redirect spending from politically popular areas – Some components of public spending like subsidies, incentives to specific sectors (agriculture, industry) created economic distortions.
- Reform the tax system – Reforms should broaden the tax base, strengthen tax collection, reduce imperfect tax incentives, and widen the overall tax base.
- Liberalise the financial sector – Williamson's recommendation here was directed at reducing the state's control over interest rates and to allow greater private sector participation in the financial sector.
- Adopt a competitive single exchange rate – Move away from over-valued exchange rates and adopt a competitive market-driven rate which reflects the true economic situation of the country.
- Reduce trade restrictions – The focus here is to reduce restrictions which favoured special interest groups within the country.
- Abolish barriers to foreign direct investment – The reasoning here being that countries will be able to access capital and technology by opening to foreign investors.

- Privatise state-owned enterprises – This recommendation pre-dates the Consensus as privatisation of inefficient state enterprises has been regarded as a litmus test of a government's commitment to step away from the economy.
- Abolish policies that restrict competition – The naïve belief in the late 1980s was that the US and Europe had near perfect market competition, which should be replicated worldwide.
- Provide secure, affordable property rights – Establishing a sound legal system which grants and upholds property rights for ownership of land, real estate, intellectual property, and business transactions.

I first read about the Consensus soon after Williamson's proposition became known in policy circles in the developing world. I was in India at the time, watching over the many distortions, inequities, and inefficiencies of the state-dominated economy. As a journalist, I recall having many conversations with business groups who felt that it was time for India to reverse economic course and embark on a Consensus-driven journey. It was part of a wave of neoliberal, free market thinking which swept the world in the 1980s.

So, what went wrong and why did the Consensus and neoliberal economics become such a toxic public policy issue in ensuing decades. It became short-hand for anyone in the developing world who had an axe to grind against American domination of the global economy and the country's handmaidens in this cause – multilateral agencies like the IMF, World Bank, and the financial system at large. In a word, it was due a combination of hubris, market ideology, and poor execution which doomed the entire enterprise from the start.

Williamson's tailored, targeted focus on Latin America was quickly forgotten, and the Consensus became *the* economic recipe which Washington-based institutions soon defined how they did business and prescribed policy solutions. What provided rocket fuel to this project was the collapse of the Soviet Union, starting with the fall of the Berlin Wall, a few months after the Williamson proposed his policy prescriptions. Economic triumphalism, talk about the end of history, and the certain death sentence of Communism and Socialism characterised that heady era in Washington D.C. and other European capitals. "We only succeed in this inter-connected world by continuing to lead the fight for free people and free and fair trade", said then President George HW Bush in a speech to Congress in December 1991.[7] "A free and prosperous global economy is essential for America's prosperity – that means jobs and economic growth right here at home".

While the President's comments were more nuanced, other commentators did not restrain themselves. The most notable of them being economist and scholar Francis Fukuyama who declared "the end of history", albeit in early 1989, several months before the formal collapse of the Soviet Union. Here is *The New Yorker* explaining Fukuyama's hypothesis over 29 years later. "Fukuyama's argument was that, with the imminent collapse of the Soviet Union, the last ideological alternative to liberalism has been eliminated". Louis Menand wrote in 2018,[8] "Fascism had been killed off in the Second World War, and now Communism was imploding. In states, like China, that called themselves Communist, political and economic reforms were heading in the direction of a liberal order". Menand goes on to explain that if you imagined history as the process by which liberal institutions – representative government, free markets, and consumerist culture – become universal, it might be possible to say that history had reached its goal. "Stuff would still happen, obviously, and smaller states could be expected to experience ethnic and religious tensions and become home to illiberal ideas". But "it matters very little what strange thoughts occur to people in Albania or Burkina Faso", Fukuyama explained, "for we are interested in what one could in some sense call the common ideological heritage of mankind".

I don't want to dwell more on Fukuyama's "end of history" thesis (there is an entire industry of scholarship and analysis out there). However, combined with the Washington Consensus, it had an astonishing impact on economic thinking during that era. The infection of these ideas was of epidemic proportions, as institutions like the World Bank and the IMF soon started fashioning their economic advice to developing countries based on Williamson's original proposition. There was a strong belief that the tide of history was irreversible, and the ten Williamson commandments constituted the only viable economic path for developing countries, individual country circumstances, and variations in economic conditions be damned. "Neoliberalism's crimes include freeing financial markets to precipitate the largest financial crisis in three-quarters of a century; freeing trade to accelerate deindustrialization: and freeing corporations to exploit consumers, workers, and the environment alike", the economist Joseph Stiglitz wrote recently,[9] with the crisis reference being with the GFC in 2008, "This form of capitalism does not enhance freedom in our society. Instead, it has led to the freedom of a few at the expense of the many. Freedom for the wolves; death for the sheep".

I want to come to Williamson's robust defence here. His thinking was not necessarily flawed, and all that the distinguished economist was doing was proposing a set of sensible economic policies, which is what economists in D.C. routinely do. The Consensus faced harsh ground realities when it touched Ground Zero – where Ivy League-trained economists working at the US Treasury, multilateral institutions (the World Bank and IMF), Wall Street, and their counterparts in large, developing nations started putting these policies into practice. The first casualty was Mexico, exemplified with the "tequila" crisis of 1994, which former IMF Managing Director Michel Camdessus prophetically described as the "first financial crisis of the 21st century".

A word about the technocratic class of that era in Washington D.C. and in countries like Mexico, Chile, Indonesia, and India. Many of them were educated in economics in elite American institutions – Berkeley, MIT, Harvard, Chicago, Yale, Princeton – being favourites. The American contingent was led by prominent economists like Larry Summers (now discredited after the Epstein saga, who was Treasury Under-Secretary when Mexico and Indonesia imploded in that decade), his boss, Treasury Secretary Robert Rubin (a Goldman Sachs alumnus), Federal Reserve Chair Alan Greenspan, and a veritable orchestra of PhD economists who served as cheerleaders.

The neoliberal, free market ideology would not have gained momentum worldwide without a technocratic army of enablers in developing nations. In Indonesia, it was the Berkeley Group of economists who spurred economic growth in that desperately poor nation in the aftermath of a bloody civil war in 1966. While the names Widjojo Nitisastro and Ali Wardhana are no longer household names in Indonesia, their Berkeley Group brought economic rigour to policymaking in Indonesia, and it yielded results for three decades. Until of course the group fell out of favour of President Suharto in the 1990s, crony capitalism became endemic, and their assistance was sought too late to deal with the severe impact of the Asian crisis on the country. In the early 1970s and in the aftermath of another coup, Chile had its fabled "Chicago boys" leading the way on economic policy. These University of Chicago-trained economists introduced orthodox thinking into economic policy, long before the Consensus was formulated, and Chile gradually transformed into an upper middle-income country under their watch. Mexico was not immune to this trend as both Presidents Carlos Salinas de Gortari (President between 1988 and 1994, Harvard MA, MPA, PhD in economics) and his successor Ernesto Zedillo (President between 1994 and 2000, Yale, MA, PhD in economics) presided over a country over-flowing with technocrats and sound economic advice. This was until the advice, built around Consensus thinking, proved to be built on a shaky foundation. In both Mexico and several East Asian nations including Indonesia, there was almost magical thinking about capital flows and exchange rates which eventually undermined economic, social, and political stability.

I was in Singapore when the *tequila* crisis unfolded in December 1994 and early 1995. There had been other financial crisis earlier in that decade – the UK's messy 1992 exit from Europe's Exchange Rate Mechanism (ERM) being a notable example. However, a crisis originating in emerging markets with a fat tail impact on peers and the markets at large was a new phenomenon. It served as a warning call to other EMs, particularly in East Asia, to fix their macroeconomic imbalances but that warning was not heeded. The root cause of the Mexican crisis had a lot to do with imperfect domestic market structures and an exchange rate pegged to the dollar. The imperfect market and exchange structure visibly manifested itself in the way foreign investors accessed short-term Mexican debt.

Here is Ted Truman,[10] a former senior US Treasury official who was in the thick of things in the run-up to the crisis. He noted that portfolio capital inflows, i.e. money invested by foreign institutions in Mexican assets, were important for Mexico and other Latin American countries at the outset of the crisis. "In the Mexican case, however, the portfolio inflows were concentrated in instruments with relatively short maturities that were also readily transferable.

> Moreover, by the time the crisis hit, a large proportion of these instruments were *tesobonos* – short-term obligations of the Mexican government whose peso value was linked to the dollar". At the end of 1993, foreigners were also large holders of *cetes* – short-term securities whose value was not linked to the dollar.

In the run up to the crisis, international investors were large holders of *tesobonos* because of the favourable interest rate differential compared with US Treasuries (debt issued by the US government). Truman says that this trend continued even after mid-1994, *when it became clear that the outstanding stock of tesobonos was larger than Mexico's foreign exchange holdings (italics mine)*. A similar saga unfolded two years later in Thailand, where the authorities were forced to devalue the baht in July 1997 when the central bank realised that it's reserves had been pledged to the forward market, which in effect meant that the country had run out of foreign exchange reserves, precipitating the Asian financial crisis.

The Mexican crisis exposed deep weaknesses in dollar-pegged exchange rate regimes, where a developing country like Thailand or Mexico or Indonesia became a hostage to the Federal Reserve's monetary policies, the latter as we know was set on purely domestic considerations. The peso and rupiah exchange had to adjust higher when the Fed's monetary stance was tighter, as was the case in the 1990s. These developing economies were ill-prepared to deal with the consequences as they consistently had to keep pace and pay higher interest rates to attract short-term foreign capital. Painful currency devaluations ensued, accompanied by sharply higher interest rates (and in some cases capital controls) to stem the flow of capital which was fleeing emerging markets at the time. While Mexico's tequila crisis in 1994 perhaps represented a tremor in the global economy, the Asian financial crisis three years later was a full-blown earthquake. Western commentators were quick to point fingers. The root cause of the crisis, we were told, was crony capitalism. Emerging markets were risky and volatile because there was an unholy relationship between business and politics, the playing field was tilted in favour of unscrupulous business interests, and political institutions were too weak to serve as a check against excess. If this comes across as an apt description of the world's largest economy today, please bear with me. As I wrote in my book on Indonesia,[11] when the Asian crisis hit in 1997, globalisation initially started off as a footnote. "Indeed, analysts were quick to blame East Asian crony capitalism – a toxic recipe which included unchecked corporate greed, unsustainable financial systems, and a political class out of touch with its people". Invidious comparisons were being drawn between fragile East Asia – with its corruption, cronyism, and weak corporate governance – and the supposedly superior institutions and governance of the west. "As we discovered this less than a decade later, Europe and America were not immune to these factors. They also suffered from cronyism, corruption, and weak corporate governance".

The global financial crisis (GFC) offered the singular lesson for America and Europe that they did not necessarily possess all the wisdom and insight in managing a modern economy and financial system. Many of the weaknesses which originally manifested itself in the emerging market crises of the 1990s also proved to be major contributors. Enough has been said and written about the origins of the GFC and its calamitous impact on the global economy. The curious thing about the GFC, however, was its relatively mild impact on the economic fortunes of the BRICS[12] economies and developing countries at large. In a research paper published by UNCTAD in 2010,[13] the authors note that "some believe that the so-called emerging economies" have turned out to be the winners of the global financial and economic crisis, in the sense that they have returned to their previous paths of high growth, whereas the leading developed economies are stuck on a slow growth path. They conclude that although the media often "exaggerate" this point, there is some truth to it.

> While the term "emerging economies" is used rather loosely, and there are no clear criteria to identify them, the share of the four BRIC countries (Brazil, Russia, India, and China) in total world production rose by roughly two percentage points, to 19.3 percent, between 2007 and 2010.

The authors note, "However, during the same period, the heterogenous group of 145 other "developing and emerging economies" also expanded its share in world GDP by two percentage points to 12.6 percent". During the same period, the share of 33 "advanced economies" (following the IMF classification) lost correspondingly four percentage points and developed country share of global output has fallen ever since.

Which brings me back to Bombay, now Mumbai, of the late 1980s when even the talk of developing countries like India and China assuming a more prominent role in the global economy was pure fantasy. Sitting at the Bombay Press Club, circa 1989, I recall fatalistic conversations with my peers about India's lost decade (the 1980s) and the dismal possibility that the next decade would amount to the same. We clearly did not see the emerging juggernaut, led by China, and were spectacularly wrong. Although that decade was characterised by several spectacular financial crisis, it also laid the foundations for the transformation of emerging markets into emerged markets, in all respects except for the most crucial one – the rules of the game was and is still unequal. We will explore how emerged markets are developing more agency and pushing back against the status quo in the next chapter.

Notes

1 I wrote about the India Growth Fund when it was launched in August 1988 – "India Growth Fund – Curtailed Ambitions", *Business India* magazine, September 5–18 1988.
2 The "taper tantrum" was an extremely volatile period for emerging markets when then Federal Reserve Governor Ben Bernanke signalled to markets that the central bank would start rolling back its unconventional monetary policy, or QE for short, which originated during the global financial crisis of 2008 (and saw the infusion of trillions of dollars of liquidity into the economy).
3 Governor Rajan spoke at the Brookings Institution in Washington D.C. on April 10, 2014. "Competitive Monetary Easing – Is it yesterday once more?".
4 "Emerging Equity Markets in The Global Economy", by John Mullin, *FRBNY Quarterly Review*, Summer 1993.
5 "Emerging Market Allocations – How Much to Own", Morgan Stanley Investment Management, report published in 2021.
6 The Washington Consensus as Policy Prescription for Development – Speech by John Williamson at the World Bank, January 13, 2004.
7 Text of President Bush's Address to Nation on Gorbachev's Resignation, December 26, 1991.
8 "Francis Fukuyama Postpones the End of History", Louis Menand, *The New Yorker*, August 27, 2018.
9 The Stiglitz quote is from his recent book *The Road to Freedom*, which was cited in a National Public Radio (NPR) blog post (May 7, 2024).
10 The Mexican Peso Crisis: Implications for International Finance, *Federal Reserve Bulletin*, March 1996.
11 Excerpt from my book "Resurgent Indonesia – From Crisis to Confidence", published in 2018. *Straits Times Press.*
12 Brazil, Russia, India, China, South Africa (BRICS) – an investment theme coined by former Goldman Sachs Chief Economist Jim O'Neill positing that large developing countries would pull away and become the engine of global growth.
13 *The Financial and Ecsssonomic Crisis of 2008–2009 and Developing Countries* – Edited by Sebastian Dullien et al., December 2010.

Chapter 2

Power

Emerged markets, often described as rising or middle powers, have developed the political spine to pursue independent and self-centred foreign policies.

The revolutionary character of our age can be summed up in three general statements: (a) the number of participants in the international order has increased and their nature has altered: (b) their technical ability to affect each other has vastly grown; c) the scope of their purposes has expanded.

If you guessed that the above quote is from master diplomat Henry Kissinger, you are right. However, you are wrong if you believe that Kissinger wrote about this in the aftermath of the Russian invasion of Ukraine. The quote is from a 1969 essay[1] he penned while serving as President Nixon's national security advisor and Secretary of State. Kissinger who passed away in November 2023 lived long enough to witness cracks in the carefully constructed Trans-Atlantic world order (of which he was both architect and cheerleader). More than any other diplomat of the post-World War era, Kissinger intimately understood the nature of power – who wields it, how it should be deployed, and the leverage which can be exercised on less powerful nations as a result.

I find it striking therefore that in the winter of his long life, Kissinger did an interview with *The Economist*,[2] where he offered a broad historical sweep of global affairs and even revised some of his earlier jaundiced views about India and its leaders. "I have very high regard for the way the Indians conduct their foreign policy now, because it shows balance", he said. This is quite the reversal of his earlier stance, circa 1971, where historical records show that he told President Nixon that the "Indians are bastards" and "they are the most aggressive goddamn people around". For good measure, Kissinger also heaped praise on the current Indian Foreign Minister Subrahmanyam Jaishankar describing him as "the practising political leader that is quite close to my views".

DOI: 10.4324/9781003603375-4

Which gives me the perfect cue to describe why a large, emerged nation like India, along with many others, broke away from conventional wisdom and the dominant Trans-Atlantic consensus on how the international community should treat Russia in the aftermath of its invasion of Ukraine in February 2022. In the hours after the Russian invasion, there was a general expectation that the international community, by and large, would roundly condemn Putin's actions for breaching international law and for encroaching upon the sovereignty of a nation state. Indeed, Article 2 (4) of the UN charter clearly sets out that all members "shall refrain in their international relations from the threat or use of force against the territorial integrity or political independence of any state, or in any manner inconsistent with the Purposes of the United Nations". In the aftermath of the invasion, the G7 imposed crippling sanctions against Russia, froze its vast foreign reserve holdings, and went after the Western business interests of Russian oligarchs. More recently, the second Trump administration has pursued a more conciliatory approach towards Moscow, while simultaneously penalising India for buying Russian oil, risking over two decades of close, strategic ties.

If the United Nations (UN) charter is so precise and clear, why did India and many others decide to pursue a dramatically different foreign policy approach? Although India did not condemn the Russian invasion, Prime Minister Modi did tell Putin that "this was not an era of war".[3] However, India continued to import huge quantities of Russian oil and gas, like China and I must add Europe, which provided the Russian economy a significant boost at a time when Moscow's access to the Western-led economic order was essentially blocked. Here is Foreign Minister Jaishankar in June 2022, four months after the invasion, being interviewed at the GLOBESEC conference in the Slovakian capital of Bratislava. He offered a radically different perspective of India's own preoccupations at the time (recovery from Covid, tensions along the border with China, the disruptive American withdrawal from Afghanistan) and the fact that the Ukraine war had led to spiralling increases in food and fuel prices, which was adversely impacting the developing world.

When pressed by the interviewer about the sharp increase in Russian oil imports into India, a contentious point for the second Trump administration, the foreign minister pointed out the obvious hypocrisy in European nations receiving a carve out for their own gas imports from the overall sanction's regime. "If you can be more considerate of yourself, surely you can be more considerate of others", he said. The session then becomes even more tense when a member of the audience conflated India's refusal to condemn the Russian invasion with the international community not coming to the rescue of New Delhi in a future conflict with China. Jaishankar's response[4] is worth reproducing in full. "If I were to take Europe collectively, which has been singularly silent on many things which were happening, for example in Asia. You can ask why anyone in Asia would trust Europe on anything at all". He added that while India had a difficult relationship with China, India was "perfectly capable of managing it". He dismissed the idea that international relations were purely transactional where one nation supports another on the expectation that mutual support would be forthcoming. The foreign minister's response was biting. "Somewhere Europe has to grow out of the mind-set that Europe's problems are the world's problems, but the world's problems are not Europe's problems. If it is you, it is yours, If it is me, it is ours". The final kicker from the foreign minister was in response to the question on whom India would side – the US or China – in case it has to pick a side. "I don't accept that India has to join either the US axis or China axis. We are one-fifth of the world's population, fifth or sixth largest economy in the world. We are entitled to weigh our own side".

Jaishankar's comments went viral, drawing praise from the emerged world, including from rival China. Here is China's *Global Times*,[5] usually a trenchant anti-Indian voice, in a laudatory commentary on the Foreign Minister's intervention at Bratislava. "So, what's most significant and interesting about the Bratislava episode was that Jaishankar – along with a mischievous smile at times – revealed the West's arrogance", the commentary noted. It added that "many Chinese netizens" saw in Jaishankar what they see in their own country.

> In a same vein, China was talked down to, cowed, pushed around, and denied the right to secure its own interests according to common sense and equality, simply because it has grown more economically prosperous and technologically advanced than what the West could tolerate.

You know that Europe has a serious problem in Asia when two competing (and sometimes warring) giants are on the same side of a major global issue. To be sure, the Ukraine invasion is not the only issue where a group of emerged powers – I would also include Indonesia and the wider Asean grouping, South Africa, Turkey, Brazil, Egypt, the UAE, and Saudi Arabia on this list –are defying conventional wisdom about global power and geopolitics. The major geopolitical trend driving this divide between the West and the rest, which I must emphasise pre-dated the Russian invasion, is in a word a lot to do with multipolarity.

To provide some historical perspective, it is helpful to look at how major powers exercised global power in the post-World War II era. This can be neatly divided into three convenient phases. The first, extending from 1945 through the collapse of the former Soviet Union, was dominated by the US and the Soviet Union. Two major nuclear powers with economic and political might competed head on for global dominance, with the rest of the world either voluntarily or coercively forced to align with either bloc. If geopolitics of that era can be likened to competing high-priced Michelin star restaurants, countries in either bloc had no choice but to accept an exhaustive 12-course chef's tasting menu with little or no flexibility on food choices. As President George W. Bush put it in a different context[6] (in the aftermath of the 9/11 terror attacks against America), "Every nation, in every region, now has a decision to make. Either you are with us, or you are with the terrorists". Substitute terrorists with anyone opposing America or the Soviet Union and you get the general idea of the geopolitical state of play until 1989.

The collapse of the former Soviet Union ushered in a unipolar world, where America was the unchallenged Sherriff in town and there was a significant reconfiguration in the world order as market rather than socialist ideology became the guiding mantra. In this setting, the world had little choice but to accept the whims and mercurial nature of the world's sole head chef. Rather than offer a refined tasting menu to patrons, the chef decided that a "take it and don't you dare leave it" approach worked best in an unchallenged environment. Cheeseburgers and freedom fries for everybody regardless of tastes or dietary restrictions. The world predictably suffered from indigestion.

While the American invasion of Afghanistan in October 2001 received broad international support it also represented a peak American power moment for geopolitics. As is the case with every major power with unlimited clout, America over-reached and the 2003 invasion of Iraq stands as a disastrous symbol of what happens when a single power literally holds the keys to the kingdom, with the ability to cajole, bully, and force nation-states to fall in line. The international community has had enough but what to do with a head chef who was in many ways indispensable for the world order? America was and is still a dominant global power, and its ability to provide global public goods – ensuring maritime security in vital sea lanes, for example, or for its ability to rally the international community in a crisis – will ensure that the country will continue to have an important role in maintaining the world order. This remains the case even with a mercurial and unpredictable current resident at the White House.

However, two significant internal developments in America since its peak power moment of 2003, which we will discuss shortly, have colluded to usher in a multipolar world order, which we are in the early stages of witnessing. In this new order, the tasting menu has been replaced by a giant buffet where countries can pick and choose who they will align with and for what cause. The buffet choice made by a country today does not necessarily connote that it will select the same food tomorrow. Countries want the freedom of choice to consume cheeseburger and French fries today, opt for a hearty Russian borscht tomorrow, and perhaps Chinese dim sum the day after. Uncle Sam, the head chef we all know too well, must share some of the cooking or accommodate other food choices where countries also express a preference for chefs Vladimir, Xi, Prabowo, Erdogan, Modi, Lula, and the rulers of the UAE and Saudi Arabia.

Looking back, the decade of the 2000s, which was marred by the 9/11 attacks and the global financial crisis (GFC), was the decade of hubris for the west. If the abiding mantra of the attacks was "why do they hate us", the principal shock from the GFC was those Western economies, just like the caricature built around emerging markets for decades, were also built on a house of sand – with dodgy financial institutions, shady financial products, and a complicit regulator veritably asleep at the wheel. I was working at the IMF during this tumultuous period, and I can say with certitude that nobody expected rich, developed nations in Europe (Ireland, Portugal, Greece, to name a few) to come to the Bretton Woods institutions, cap in hand, for financial assistance.

If the 2000s represented a decade of setbacks for the west, the opposite was the case for emerged markets, where it was a decade of expansion and opportunity. Starting with China's accession to the World Trade Organisation (WTO), a sore point for American policymakers who believe that Beijing was handed access to the global economy with very little strings attached, the decade saw sustained economic growth in much of the emerged world. China also triggered a commodity super-cycle after it expanded fiscal stimulus, worth $568 billion or a whopping 13% of GDP, as a way of restoring confidence and growth in the global economy. The country's insatiable appetite for commodities ranging from soybeans to beef, iron ore to copper, restored economic growth in much of the emerged world with Indonesia, Argentina, and Brazil being principal beneficiaries. The 2000s was also the decade of the restoration of the G20, which brought together nations which accounted for over 80% of global output, and the emergence of the BRICS (both of which we will discuss in a subsequent chapter) as an investment proposition (with mixed results) as well to organise and to project geopolitical power. Despite these achievements, the rest of the emerged world still felt that it was forced to play as a B-team because the G7 controlled all the levers of global power. Something snapped with the Russian invasion of Ukraine.

Fiona Hill, a senior fellow at the Brookings Institution, captured the sentiment of the "rest" very well in a speech[7] she delivered in 2023. She said that it was not just Russia that seeks to push the US to the sidelines in Europe but also China that wants to minimise and contain US military and economic presence in Asia so both can secure their respective spheres of influence. "Other countries that have traditionally been considered 'middle powers' or 'swing states' – the so-called 'Rest' of the world – seek to cut the US down to a different size in their neighbourhoods and exert more influence in global affairs. They want to decide, not be told what's in their interest. In short, in 2023, we hear a resounding no to US domination and see a marked appetite for a world without a hegemon". Hill was even more trenchant in her analysis that the "Global South"[8] feels constantly marginalised in world affairs. "Why in fact are they labelled the 'Global South', having previously been called the Third World or Developing World? Why are they even the 'Rest' of the world? They *are* the world, representing 6.5 billion people. Our terminology reeks of colonialism".

Hill is not the only geopolitical expert who is deeply sceptical about the long-term durability of the American-led world order. As early as 2013, Singapore diplomat Kishore Mahbubani was warning[9] about Americans being singularly unprepared if the "world's centre of gravity shifts to Asia". Americans needed to be told a simple, mathematical truth, Mahbubani warned. "With 3% of the world's population, the US can no longer dominate the rest of the world, because Asians, with 60% of the world's population, are no longer underperforming". He added that while Americans tend to receive only good news, Asia's rise is not really bad news.

> The US should recognise that Asian countries are seeking not to dominate the West, but to emulate it. They seek to build strong and dynamic middle classes and to achieve the kind of peace, stability, and prosperity that the West has long enjoyed.

Mahbubani's views represents the Asian and unabashedly Chinese perspective of how the world should be governed in a multipolar world.

Similarly, Brazilian President Lula Inacio Lula da Silva, who has also refused to condemn the Russian invasion of Ukraine, has championed global governance reforms as a way for addressing the power imbalance between the West and the rest.

> We cannot wait for another global tragedy, like the Second World War, to build a new global governance over its ruins. The will of the majority can persuade those who cling to the crude expressions of the mechanisms of power.

The President thundered at his speech to the UN General Assembly in September 2024. Which brings me back to the head chef America and how it sees its evolving global role. I must emphasise that most external analyses of America's evolving superpower role are built on a combination of fanciful ideology and wishful thinking. I agree that a multipolar world order requires America to cede more power and recognise that the emerged world deserves greater global power and privileges. At the same time,

America is not about to voluntarily vacate its global role despite internal challenges like a febrile democracy, greater nationalism, and a diminished fiscal ability and appetite to embark on global military adventures.

The facts don't stack up. It is truly astonishing that in 2023 and 2024, while the Chinese economy stumbled after a prolonged period of economic expansion (which was unprecedented in history), the American economy charged ahead with growth rates described by *The Economist*[10] as being the "envy of the world".

> On a per-person basis, American economic output is now about 40% higher than in western Europe and Canada, and 60% higher than in Japan – roughly twice as large as the gaps between them in 1990. Average wages in America's poorest state, Mississippi, are higher than the averages in Britain, Canada, and Germany.

In good measure, the magazine noted that China's output per person remains less than a third of America's; India is "smaller still". Yet the size of China and India's economies should not be under-estimated. With a GDP more than $16 trillion, China is the second largest economy in the world and India's own economy recently surpassed that of the UK, it's former colonial master. The emerged world is catching up but trails America by a large measure.

The principal question for Trump's America is whether it wishes to exert global influence at the same size and scope as it has done for the last several decades. None of this comes cheap. American defence spending in 2023, at 3.5% of GDP or $900 billion, accounted for 40% of the global total. China, by contrast, spent around 2% of its GDP or around $300 billion during the same year. The annual budget of America's intelligence community in 2024 was around $73 billion alone, slightly smaller than India's annual defence spending and at about the same level as that country's trade deficit with China. The rise of Trump has ushered in an introspective period in America, with most of the population fretting about basic kitchen table issues – the cost of living, social devastation from the migration of manufacturing jobs to China, Mexico, and other parts of the emerged world. Kishore Mahbubani and other scholars have argued that this is perhaps an opportune moment for America to step back from the global stage. "I would encourage Americans...to first take care of America's own internal problems before trying to transform the world", he told China's principal news agency *Xinhua*.[11] This is a disingenuous statement, to say the least, given America's economic strength and power projection abilities across the globe. It is true that America must, sooner or later, wrestle with pressing domestic issues like an unsustainable fiscal deficit, rising social challenges (polarisation, the scrouge of gun violence) and the simple fact that much of its population appears disinterested in the country's status as a world power.

Through history, the British empire included, the nation with superpower status has almost always had to struggle with the domestic costs of foreign adventures and misadventures. Power and influence do not recede at the switch of a button. At the height of its power and influence just before World War I, Britain dominated the global economy like no other nation at the time. Although it suffered crippling financial setbacks because of the cost of financing the first war and subsequent withdrawal from the gold standard (during the Great Depression era of the early 1930s), the country retained its influence well through the 1950s until the humiliating Suez crisis. If Mahbubani's argument is to be taken to its logical extension, perhaps it is time for China to also focus on its own internal problems (a rapidly ageing population, lack of adequate safety nets, and a decrepit property sector) rather than expend trillions of dollars in lending via the Belt Road Initiative (BRI) and to give up attempts to build strategic influence in many parts of the world. The important lesson here is that in a multipolar world, there will be *multiple* nodes of power and influence, including of course America and China.

Taking a contrarian view, a Norwegian foreign policy scholar has argued that the world is *not* multipolar. "The reasons are straightforward", Jo Inge Bekkevold writes.[12]

> Polarity simply refers to the number of great powers in the international system – and for the world to be multipolar, there have to be three or more such powers. Today, there are only two countries with the economic size, military might, and global leverage to constitute a pole: the United States and China.

Other great powers are nowhere in sight, he argues, and they won't be anytime soon. "The mere fact that there are rising middle powers and nonaligned countries with large populations and growing economies does not make the world multipolar".

Bekkevold is right if you apply traditional theories of geopolitics – where an incumbent power has almost inevitably been challenged by a rising one, with the US and China serving as the latest instalment in that centuries-old saga. While the US-China contest does represent the most profound geopolitical challenge of this generation, the evidence is overwhelming that the rest of the world is not a passive bystander in dealing with conflicts in their backyard. Rising middle or regional powers illustrated in this chapter, notably India, Saudi Arabia, Turkey, and the UAE are building their own theatres of geopolitical influence and the US appears content not to overtly interfere in these regional flareups.

The rising middle powers are divided into three broad categories when it comes to engagement with the west and intentions to replace the existing order. China, along with Russia, Iran, and North Korea, belongs to the *hard* anti-west category, where the objective of Beijing and its junior partners is to gradually build a new world order. China prides continuity and global stability above everything else and periodically attempts to rein in Russia and others from seeking to disrupt the status quo. However, China's intentions are very clear and articulated in the three global initiatives launched by Xi in recent years, addressing development, security, and civilisation.

The second category of middle powers are countries in the *light* anti-west grouping, Turkey and Brazil stand out here, they recognise that the existing system has its merits (and therefore should not be dismantled) but want to exercise greater leverage and power projection in their respective backyards. Under President Lula, Brazil has forged closer ties with China, Russia, and other members of the BRICS, complaining at times about the continued dominance of the US dollar. Turkey, under President Erdogan's mercurial leadership, blows hot and cold with the west depending on the geopolitical issue at hand. As a member of NATO, Turkey is obliged to participate in any external operation if the charter's Article 5 is triggered.[13] However, Turkey has forged a more independent and assertive foreign policy which places the country at odds with NATO from time to time.

The final category brings together India, Indonesia/Asean, the UAE, and Saudi Arabia – their foreign policy approach can best be labelled as being *non-west*. These countries not only want to support the existing order and reform it from within but also wish to exercise greater autonomy in how they deal with the world. This partially explains India's tilt towards Russia in the ongoing conflict with Ukraine and continued participation in America-mandated regional arrangements such as the Quad and the now defunct IPEF. Similarly, both Saudi Arabia and the UAE have vastly expanded their economic relations with China and Russia in recent years. However, when it came to making a hard choice, where the UAE, for example, had to pick a side on continued cooperation on AI, Abu Dhabi decisively moved in favour of the American side.[14]

The regional adventures of the middle powers (or more aptly should be described as *misadventures)* should be viewed in this context. When Turkey intervened in 2020 in support of Azerbaijan, which eventually wrested control over disputed territory from neighbouring Armenia, the international community expressed generic concern about the escalation in violence. However, both the US and China did not expend diplomatic capital by directly intervening in the resolution of the conflict, which was settled in Azerbaijan's favour because of Turkey's strong advocacy. It was the second Trump administration which belatedly brought Azerbaijan and Armenia together to sign a peace accord. In a previous era, the UN Security Council would have huffed and puffed and threaten to deploy peacekeepers to contain the conflict. International institutions like the UN are simply exhausted and unable to mediate or intervene in regional conflicts. The evidence is even stronger when one considers the troika of regional conflicts in the Middle East and North Africa, involving Syria, Yemen, Sudan, and Libya, where middle powers have been prominent and promiscuous in direct intervention. Much has already been written about Syria and let me focus instead on Yemen and Libya.

Yemen's civil war, as the Council on Foreign Relations (CFR)[15] explains, started in 2014 when Houthi insurgents, with the explicit backing of Iran, took control of Yemen's capital Sanaa, ostensibly demanding lower fuel prices and a new government. Following failed negotiations, the rebels seized the presidential palace in January 2015, leading President Hadi and his government to resign. "Beginning in March 2015, a coalition of Gulf states led by Saudi Arabia launched a campaign of economic isolation and air strikes against the Houthi insurgents, ***with U.S. logistical and intelligence support (bold italics mine)***".

The US was content until recently to outsource resolution of this regional conflict to its Gulf allies, although this is essentially a proxy war with Iran, which has vastly expanded its regional influencing efforts by supporting Hezbollah in Lebanon, the Houthis in Yemen, and Hamas in Gaza. The humanitarian consequences of the conflict are horrific. The UN estimates that 60% of the estimated 377,000 deaths between 2015 and the beginning of 2022 were the "result" of indirect causes like food insecurity and lack of accessible health services. Two-thirds of the population, or 21.6 million Yemenis, remain in dire need of assistance. Five million are at the risk of famine, and a cholera outbreak has affected over 1 million people. "All sides of the conflict are reported to have violated human rights and international humanitarian law" according to the CFR report. Would more direct American or even Chinese or multilateral intervention, going by conventional rules of geopolitics, have helped in minimising the awful humanitarian impact of the conflict? The depressing answer from Washington D.C. and New York is that both the incumbent and rising superpower, and the world's premier conflict mediation organisation seem content with the status quo and have little appetite to be dragged into a prolonged regional conflict, with serious geopolitical consequences, as the 2023 Houthi attacks on Red Sea shipping have demonstrated. Unless, of course, it directly harms the US, economic interests, as the Houthi blockade of vital Red Sea shipping lanes in 2023 and 2024 demonstrated, which resulted in repeated US air strikes and a tentative agreement where the Houthis agreed to stop the attacks. The subsequent US and Israeli targeted bombing of Iranian nuclear sites was also aimed at reining in the regional power. However, this scattershot intervention will do little to address deeper, long-standing causes of the conflict.

This state of apathy (and delegation of responsibility to middle powers) has become even more acute in the case of Libya, a failed state in North Africa which has struggled mightily since dictator Muammar Gadaffi was ousted in 2011. The oil-rich country has splintered between warring factions and best illustrates the Obama administration's "leading from behind"[16] approach, which has failed miserably. The major powers currently involved in Libya's ongoing civil war are Russia, Turkey, and the UAE. In the nine-year conflict, as *The Guardian* reported, Turkey backed the internationally recognised government in Tripoli with troops and weapons, while the UAE has bolstered opposing forces in eastern Libya led by General Khalifa Haftar. After a protracted escalation in hostilities during the pandemic, Turkey and the UAE patched up their differences. This has not necessarily led to a cessation in hostilities due to the presence of Russia's Wagner Group, which is fighting on the side of General Haftar, extending the mercenary group's reach and influence from Libya into Africa's Sahel region, which has been bristling with instability as a direct result of the conflict in Libya. Why are regional powers so interested in getting involved in Libya and how do they define national interest? The Soufan Centre offers a less than benevolent reason for their involvement. "Despite the steps taken to promote the rule of law in western Libya, the continuing nationwide duality of power enables regional and global powers to strike separate agreements with the two rivals to advance their own interests"; the Centre argued in an Intel Brief,[17]"In so doing, the outside powers have established lucrative business and illicit arrangements that enable the two Libyan administrations to flourish separately, reducing their urgency to forge a united political and economic whole".

Very much the same impulse appears to be driving the civil war in neighbouring Sudan, where the official Sudan Army, backed by Saudi Arabia, is waging a bloody civil war against the rival Rapid Support Forces (RSF), ostensibly backed by the UAE, which has denied any involvement. The battle between the rival generals involved in the conflict, Abdel Fattah al-Burhan of the Sudan's official army and Mohamed Hamdan Dagalo (also known as Hemeti), of the RSF, has already claimed over 150,000 lives, 2 million displaced, and horrific reports of human rights abuses.

> Sudan is a bridge that links the Middle East and Africa, and its abundant natural resources mean the battle for Khartoum has taken on a regional dimension. Gulf heavyweights Saudi Arabia and the UAE view the war as a chance to cement their hegemonic status in the Middle East,

according to Talal Mohammad,[18] an associate fellow at the Royal United Services Institute.

The involvement of middle powers in escalating regional conflict raises several questions about the global order, which US hegemony over several decades was meant to protect. While human rights abuses cannot be defended, is there a more benign reason why the middle powers feel compelled to expend blood and treasure to protect their regional interests? More fundamentally, does the rise of middle powers also signal that some problems are best resolved by countries with contiguous geographies with the regions in conflict? It is undeniable that some of the jockeying for regional supremacy in North Africa has a lot to do with the diffusion of American power in recent years. This has not only emboldened the middle powers to directly intervene, something which they would not have countenanced during an earlier era of American unipolarity. A confusing aspect of US foreign policy is its continued unconditional commitment to protecting Europe (as evidenced by the huge financial support for Ukraine in its war against Russia, although that support looks shaky in the second Trump administration) and with Israel in its conflict with Gaza and Lebanon. There is an argument that American support for Europe is both for historic, benevolent reasons (originating from the end of World War II) and in countering Russia's growing influence. Yet as Indian Foreign Minister Jaishankar pointed out at Bratislava, the Ukraine conflict is perhaps a peculiarly European problem best dealt with at the regional level.

There are also contradictions galore in how the incumbent and middle powers are viewing the state of the world and taking protective action. C. Rajamohan, one of India's foremost strategic thinkers, said in a prescient speech in 2013[19] that Asian middle powers were becoming more assertive because they are nervous about the trajectory of US-China tensions, which is taking place in their backyard.

> Therefore, the question is – how do we insure against the twists and turns in the US-China relationship? Are we going to be merely responding to the ups and downs of that relationship, or do we ensure by doing more cooperation between ourselves so that we can create a framework that, like a shock absorber, can take some pressure off the twists and turns in the US-China relationship,

he said. In positioning themselves to absorb the worst effects of a US-China conflict, Asian middle powers are taking a common view that they don't want to be forced into making "invidious choices",[20] in the words of Singapore Foreign Minister Vivian Balakrishnan, of picking a side in this superpower tussle.

There are several benign reasons why the emerged powers should have a greater say in how global conflicts should be managed. There is also a full suite of global challenges, notably combating climate change, where regional and local solutions will have the highest impact. As we will discuss in the next chapter, the emerged powers are also deploying capital and technology into the developing world as part of their calculated strategy to build regional influence.

Notes

1 *Foreign Relations of the United States, 1969–1976, Volume 1, Foundations of Foreign Policy, 1968–1972*– Essay by Henry Kissinger, 1969.
2 Henry Kissinger explains how to avoid World War III – Kissinger interview with *The Economist* –May 17, 2023.
3 The Prime Minister's full quote is as follows: "I have said directly and publicly, this is not an era of war" which he said he conveyed to President Putin "but it is one of dialogue and diplomacy and we must do what we can to stop the bloodshed and human suffering".
4 India'sForeignMinisterS.JaishankaratGlobesec2022,Bratislava.Thevideocanbe accessed at www.youtube.com/live/m_UH3jWfH28?si+ASATKAltURJKzOmY.
5 Why did Jaishankar's speech suddenly become popular in China –*Global Times*, June 9, 2022.
6 President George W. Bush – Address to a Joint Session of Congress, September 20, 2001.
7 Fiona Hill – Lennart Mari Lecture 2023.
8 Full disclosure – this is a label I absolutely detest and will not use it in the rest of the book.
9 America's Blinders – by Kishore Mahbubani, Project Syndicate, May 24, 2013.
10 The Economist, Special Report – The American economy has left other rich countries in the dust, October 14, 2024.
11 Interview: Singaporeans scholar urges the US to abandon outdated strategic mentality – Xinhua, May 17, 2021.
12 No, the World is not Multipolar – Jo Inge Bekkevold, Foreign Policy, September 22, 2023.
13 This requires all NATO members to step in if a member is attacked, treating it as an attack on themselves.
14 For more on G42, the Abu Dhabi AI company, which has inked a partnership with Microsoft, read "G42 and the China-UAE-US triangle, The Washington Post, April 3, 2024.
15 Conflict in Yemen and the Red Sea – Center for Preventive Action, CFR, Updated on October 8, 2024.
16 A White House official is believed to have coined the phrase in 2011, when the US allowed France and the UK to lead on the aftermath of Gadaffi's brutal ouster. It has instead become a metaphor for American disinterest in getting involved in regional conflicts.
17 Outside Powers Exploit Libya's Divisions – Soufan Centre, March 6, 2024.
18 How Sudan Became a Saudi-UAE Proxy War – Foreign Policy, July 12, 2023.
19 Lowy Lecture Series: "Indo-Pacific balancing act – in search of a middle power coalition" – Lecture by Dr. Rajamohan, 23 October 2013.
20 Speech by Vivian Balakrishnan at CSIS, Washington D.C., May 15, 2019.

Chapter 3

Capital

Capital used to originate in the west. It now also flows south to south, east to east.

When I moved from India to Singapore in 1990, I felt like I had stepped into a time machine well into the future. It was not just Singapore's impressive infrastructure and squeaky-clean reputation which captivated me. The notion that an Asian city-state, not far from India's shores, had made it from Third World to First in my lifetime was a sight to behold. I was a financial reporter for a local business newspaper at the time, and this was a fascinating vantage point to observe and understand the "secret sauce" of Singapore's dramatic rise. The city-state had just celebrated its silver jubilee as an independent nation, and the leadership made bold prognostications about the next 25 years.

Schooled as I was in the traditional rhetoric deployed by politicians in a noisy democracy, it was shocking to see that Singapore's leadership not only had a long-term economic vision but had set aside the financial resources to back that ambition.

As it is in many parts of the world today, investing in the future is a nice, pithy talking point. In Singapore, the rhetoric was backed by cold cash, mainly originating from returns generated by two giant sovereign wealth funds (SWFs) – the Government of Singapore Investment Corporation (GIC) and Temasek Holdings. When the Singapore authorities established Temasek in 1974, its foundational holdings were in three dozen or so local companies hitherto owned by the Finance Ministry. "The objective behind Temasek's establishment was to distance the government, with its role as policymaker, from its role as shareholder", the former President of Singapore S.R. Nathan recalled in 2004.[1] Seven years after Temasek's founding, the government took another bold step in 1981 by establishing GIC, primarily to manage Singapore's growing foreign reserves. It is important to emphasise that Singapore was still a fledgeling developing

DOI: 10.4324/9781003603375-5

nation when Temasek and GIC were established. Until that time, it was only oil-rich nations which established early versions of SWFs, to reinvest the huge surpluses from the spike in oil prices in the 1970s. Neighbouring Brunei established the Brunei Investment Agency in 1983, and the Kuwait Investment Authority (KIA) were trend-setters, although it soon developed a reputation for misgovernance and questionable investments. What made Singapore stand apart was the fact that its investible resources did not originate from fossil fuels, understandable since the city-state had none of it, but was wisely redeploying current account surpluses to build a global investment portfolio. Today the two Singapore SWFs are giants, with Temasek's net portfolio value at around $288 billion according to latest data and informal estimates place GICs total assets at around $770 billion.[2] Over the years, I have heard significantly higher estimates running into $1 trillion or more. In its annual report, GIC only discloses the average annual return it has generated on its investment portfolio, which in 2023 it placed at 4.6% over the last two decades.

It is mind boggling that a non-oil city-state with an annual GDP of around $530 billion has salted away savings equivalent to around 300% of GDP in a matter of decades. When Singapore started on this journey in the early 1970s, it was an anomaly in the investment world. Capital only flowed west to east, north to south and it was mainly in the form of concessional aid and some foreign direct investment (FDI). The quaint thought that a tiny developing nation located on the other side of the planet could set aside funds for the future generated a fair share of laughter, just as Japan's foray into exporting automobiles to the developed west a decade earlier. Singapore approached the task methodically, recruiting qualified fund managers and placing good governance as a top priority. Even today, the Prime Minister of Singapore serves as Chair of the investment fund, providing a direct link between public accountability and generating adequate returns. Former GIC President Lim Chow Kiat[3] has described the investment fund's successful approach as "enduring short-term uncertainty, and occasional short-term pain". He said that over the years, GIC has learnt that it is not the time horizon that matters most but rather the "mind-set and discipline to consistently invest based on fundamentals".

Today the quaint anomaly which was once GIC has become a startling global reality as several surplus-rich emerged nations have established investment funds, or SWFs, to invest for the long term. As can be expected, some of them have been incredibly successful in fulfilling their mandate, while many others are saddled with political interference and poor investment decisions. The macro picture first. The Global SWF Data Platform[4] estimates that in developed and emerged markets, the grouping of state-owned investors – which includes SWFs, pension funds, and central banks – managed an astonishing $55 trillion in 2024. Understandably,

America and Europe feature in this list but their share of the total pile is no longer dominant. Globally, central banks had around $16.9 trillion in reserves with the Asian and Middle Eastern share accounting for a dominant 80%. Similarly, of the estimated $12.9 trillion in assets under management held by SWFs, the Asian and Middle Eastern share amounted to an equally dominant 75% of the total. It is only in the public pension fund category ($25 trillion aum), where America and Europe dominate. To provide a sense of the sheer scale of the Middle Eastern SWFs, consider Abu Dhabi's pile of $1.67 trillion (which is slightly out-matched by Norway's $1.68 trillion), Saudi Arabia's Public Investment Fund ($1.19 trillion), and other holdings of assorted Gulf sheikhdoms (Dubai – $490 billion: Kuwait – $978 billion: Qatar – $590 billion). These dizzying statistics are complemented by foreign reserve holdings of China (estimated $2 trillion) and Hong Kong ($1 trillion), which is primarily deployed to maintain the HKD's peg to the US dollar) and other Asian countries. Away from the SWF space, a major new disrupter in the development aid space has been China, as it expanded its global aid footprint and reach over the past decade, with mixed results. These investment funds are demonstrating their investment might – by deploying capital in the advanced west and increasingly in the emerged world. GIC and Temasek have proven to be savvy investors in China and India, for example, and the UAE has become one of the largest foreign investors in Africa.

Capital is flowing east to east, south to south for the first time in our modern era. There are two additional factors at play which is facilitating this trend. First, global remittances from developed to the emerged world has surged because of the presence of foreign workers and immigrants in the rich world, including Gulf nations, Japan, and the Asian tigers. The World Bank estimates that global remittances were estimated to have grown by 4.6% in 2024 to a phenomenal $905 billion. The Bank's Dilip Ratha,[5] who is a well-known expert on the subject, estimates that the top five recipient countries for remittances were India ($129 billion), followed by Mexico ($68 billion), China ($48 billion), the Philippines ($40 billion), and Pakistan ($33 billion). "It is notable that remittances have continued to outpace other types of external financial flows to low-to-middle income countries. Remittances have even surpassed FDI significantly" according to Ratha.

For countries like India, Mexico, and the Philippines, remittances have become a reliable source of foreign exchange inflows, which bolsters the balance of payments and makes additional financial resources available for the recipient country. Some countries, notably in Africa, have also raised money through so-called "diaspora bonds", where wealthier immigrants invest in foreign currency bonds issued by the central bank or finance ministry. A second reason why the emerged world has, well, emerged financially stronger is their ability to raise domestic revenue and the development of their capital markets. Very low ratios of tax-to-GDP were a scourge on the emerged world for decades, impairing their ability to invest for the long term and prolonging their dependence on aid flows to match domestic revenue shortfalls.

In the BRICS grouping, Brazil is a standout with a tax-to-GDP ratio of more than 32% in 2024 (not far from the OECD average of around 34%) with other countries following with lower but significantly rising ratios. Higher levels of domestic revenue mobilisation have enabled the emerged world to invest for the long term – in physical infrastructure, health, and education.

A major enabler of this surge in investment has also been due to the increasing maturity and sophistication of capital markets. China/Hongkong and India alone have a combined market capitalisation in excess of $22 trillion, smaller compared with America's $60 trillion but a significant number, nevertheless. As context, I must also add that the combined market cap of Germany, the UK, and France works out to around $9 trillion as I write this. You can be a better judge on who qualifies for the emerging markets label.

The availability of liquid, deep capital markets in the emerged world has seen the rise of private sector giants like China's Tencent, Brazil's Bank Itau, India's Reliance, Korea's Hyundai, and Singapore's DBS Bank. These corporates have been able to reliably raise capital at home, thanks to the growth of a strong domestic investor class, while simultaneously being able to global markets. They literally are enjoying the best of both worlds.

To step back in time, when the Asian financial crisis decimated the economies of Korea and South-East Asia in the late 1990s, policymakers in the region drew two important lessons. First, countries were essentially on their own, notwithstanding massive assistance from the IMF (which came with uncomfortable strings attached). Second, the only way to insure against future crises was for countries to accumulate massive dollar reserves, often to their detriment (it kept their economies tied to trade and investment and suppressed domestic demand). This explains why India feels the need to hold $700 billion in reserves (bolstered by remittances) and Indonesia, which was at the epicentre of the Asian crisis, to keep $152 billion in rainy day dollar holdings.

We will address the contentious topic of the role of the dollar in a subsequent chapter and potential competitors looking to displace the greenback. However, the overwhelming message from this torrent of reserve holdings and capital originating from emerged markets is obvious – the developed world is no longer the sole provider of portfolio and investment flows, and indeed of concessional finance, if China and India's growing appetite is factored in. Where is this money being deployed and what lessons, positive and negative, can we glean from the surge in eastern capital? It can all be categorised under the puzzling, the confounding, and the good.

The obvious place to start with is the puzzling – China's Belt Road Initiative (BRI) which represents an extreme example of a competing superpower attempting to dramatically transform the rules of the foreign aid and investment game. The BRI started in 2013 with benign intentions. Low-income countries in Africa, which relied on Western development aid for several decades, were starved of investment capital to build infrastructure. From my time at the IMF, I recall furious debates within the Organisation for Economic Co-operation and Development (OECD) grouping on the nature and composition of aid flows into sub-Saharan Africa (SSA) in the two decades straddling 1990 and 2000. There was a philosophical belief in the west that low-income SSA countries required a cocktail of external support which included a blend of debt relief, concessional finance which was directed mainly at budget support, and a tacit encouragement for more stable countries in the grouping to also access international capital markets with bond issues.

For me at the time, Uganda stood out as a country which epitomised why the OECD approach was flawed to begin with. At one stage in the mid-2000s, Uganda relied on Western aid for around 60% by way of general budget support i.e. external assistance was essentially keeping the government afloat, with little room for longer term capital expenditure. The substantial debt relief which Uganda received did create fiscal space in scaling expenditure on health and education. But these benefits were short-lived, as a significant debt crisis unfolded a decade or so later. At the time Uganda was being held up as a good example of Western aid intervention, the country's leadership (and increasingly Beijing, which was turning its attention towards providing development assistance) was seeking alternative models of aid.

When Xi Jinping became President in 2012, he immediately sought to change two abiding aspects of China's foreign policy approach. The first rule which he over-turned was to be more assertive in advocating China's role on the global stage, dismantling Deng Xiaoping's famous call for the country to lie low. "Hide your strength, bide your time, never take the lead", the late Chinese leader told his party colleagues.[6] Xi over-turned the central plank of how China interacted with the world and just like Mao has proven to be a disruptive and transformative leader, for better and worse. The BRI stands out as a towering symbol of Xi's global ambitions and of hubris. It also represents Beijing's trillion-dollar folly.

At its heart, the BRI attempted to recalibrate the global aid architecture with an audacious plan to supplant the Western-led OECD offering. As China's State Council Information Office[7] notes, President Xi proposed the "vision of a global community of shared future" in September and October 2013.

> The Belt and Road Initiative (BRI) is a creative development that takes on and carries forward the spirit of the ancient silk routes – two of the

great achievements in human history and civilization. It enriches the ancient spirit with the zeitgeist and culture of the new era and provides a platform for building a global community of a shared future.

I was working at an international bank with vast China operations at the time. My initial reaction was positive. Developing countries desperately needed infrastructure for long-term development, and traditional sources of aid were drying up. European countries were struggling to meet their self-directed aid target of 0.7% of GDP, with the UK and Scandinavian nations the only ones poised to breach that threshold. I must add that the UK has since sharply cut back that target.

The private sector was largely AWOL in Africa as well. International banks bemoaned the lack of "bankable projects" in SSA, short hand for low-risk financing where the commercial prospects for recovering principal and interest were bright. After a sustained period of attention and financing, the Western-led OECD grouping was forced to reduce development assistance due to fiscal pressures from the global financial crisis (GFC).

Moreover, recipient countries felt that while levels of assistance were tapering off, Western leaders were still preachy when it came to offering solicited and unsolicited advice. As Larry Summers noted recently[8]: "Somebody from a developing country said to me, what we get from China is an airport. What we get from the United States is a lecture". This was precisely the opening which Xi was looking for, positioning China as a reliable and non-preachy partner for development and a role model. There is of course considerable merit in developing countries emulating China's development approach. There is no precedent in history of a country of the size of China transforming itself from dirt poor to solid middle-income status in a generation. China's command and control approach towards economic planning, a ruthless focus on implementation and outcomes, and for pursuing a non-Marxist tilt in integrating itself to the global economy are textbook examples for many developing nations. It therefore came as a shock that when it came to implementing the BRI on a grand global sale, none of these positive attributes were visible. In scope and scale, BRI reminds me more of America's sub-prime mortgage debacle rather than the ruthless efficiency that we have come to associate China's policymakers and their implementation abilities.

The comparison with sub-prime mortgages is not overstated. To quickly recap, here is how the American think-tank Center for American Progress[9] describes the genesis and impact of the US sub-prime mortgage crisis. In the period leading up to the 2008 GFC, which had its origins in the distress in the housing market, purely private mortgage providers (called the private label securities market or PLS for short) supplanted the traditional financing role of US government and so-called government-sponsored enterprises (GSEs) (Fannie Mae and other mortgage packagers and guarantors).

Despite their controversial role as state-owned entities in a rapaciously free enterprise housing market, the participation of the GSEs provided a semblance of stability to the housing market. I am not suggesting here that the OECD played a similar role in the provision of aid and development assistance to low-income countries as the comparison is far-fetched, mainly because the OECD and multilateral institutions also committed their fair share of blunders in Africa (anyone remembers the ill-fated 1980s when structural adjustment was the buzz word?).

The CAP report on the sub-prime crisis notes that the entry of a purely "private label securities market" had catastrophic consequences for the American economy.

> During this period, there was a dramatic expansion in mortgage lending, a large portion of which was in sub-prime loans with predatory features. Most of this mortgage lending was to existing homeowners refinancing, with many believing that they were taking advantage of lower interest rates to extract home equity,

the report says. Instead, these homeowners were often exposed to complex and risky products that quickly became unaffordable when economic conditions changed. "Linked with the expansion of predatory lending and the growth of the private PLS market was the repackaging of these risky loans into complicated products through which the same assets were sold multiple times throughout the financial system".

Let me briefly come to China's defence with BRI. It was launched with the benign intention of exporting the China development model with the added incentive of providing cheap, many-strings-attached financing to build infrastructure. Sadly, the China we have grown to admire and respect was nowhere in sight when it came to actual BRI lending, where an estimated $1 trillion or more in financing flowed in the ten-year period between 2013 and 2023. The lending by Chinese state-owned and commercial entities was uncoordinated with conflicting objectives and the heavy hand of China's foreign policy goal of advancing its global interest all too visible. Researchers at Chatham House,[10] where I am affiliated, argued in a contrarian research paper in 2020 that the portrayal of the BRI as a China-sponsored "geopolitical strategy that ensnares countries in unsustainable debt and allows China undue influence" is a flawed construct. "China's development financing system is too fragmented and poorly coordinated to pursue detailed strategic objectives: and developing country governments and economic interests determine the nature of BRI projects on their territory". The research paper has not travelled well as it was published during the pandemic, just around the time that many BRI-recipient countries reported high levels of debt distress.

Worse, in many of the infrastructure projects it funded in Africa, China insisted that its own workforce be deployed to carry out the profound task of project planning and the more mundane job of paving the roads and polishing the marble. This implies some level of central coordination and policy design. At a bar in Kigali, Rwanda, sometime in 2012, I encountered a group of at least 15 Chinese workers who had been shipped in from Shenzhen to help with a hotel project. It is truly astonishing that a country which routinely invokes a "century of humiliation" which it suffered under colonial rule has forgotten those lessons. For the Zambian plumber or Tanzanian welder, it must have been equally humiliating to see their livelihoods undermined as Chinese expatriates assumed many of the tasks in a major project.

Sadly, when it came to the resolution of these debt distress cases in the aftermath of the pandemic, China has strangely taken a hands-off approach, asserting that a significant portion of BRI loans was provided by Chinese commercial entities, not the state. With my friend and colleague Jeremy Mark, I have extensively chronicled China's torturous attempts to stall debt restructuring negotiations with low-income countries. In February 2023, we wrote[11] that the IMF estimated that 60% of low-income countries are in, or at high risk of, debt distress – double the 2015 level. Yet a global framework for debt resolution was not working because of foot-dragging by the private sector and China.

> While the private sector hopes to extract favourable terms by way of debt repayments or an outright haircut, China's position is more ambivalent: Geopolitics plays a role, and Beijing prefers having leverage over countries in debt distress. The result is an international community which cannot deliver.

Lest you conclude that *all* emerged countries are pursuing the China BRI model, let me emphasise that India is playing a far more constructive role, albeit on a smaller scale. In Sri Lanka, India stepped in with $4 billion in financing at the height of economic distress in 2023 and quietly aligned with the IMF and World Bank when it came to resolution of that debt. In a rare slight to China's BRI approach and recalcitrance on debt negotiations, India's G20 Sherpa Amitabh Kant took on Beijing during the country's chairing of the global body.

> "China needs to come out openly and say what their debt is and how to settle it" Kant said "It can't be that the IMF takes a haircut, and it goes to settle Chinese debt. How is that possible? Everybody has to take a haircut."

This proves there is a sensible path for emerged countries when it comes to providing development finance to other developing countries.

If China represents the puzzling, even ugly aspect of capital flows east to east (which hopefully it will rectify under a retooled BRI 2.0), let's turn to the confounding. Ground Zero of bad SWF investing is surely in central London, where trophy property asset after trophy property asset has been accumulated in recent years by the Qatar Investment Authority (QIA) (assets under management $590 billion) and allied agencies. There is a bizarre fascination for London property held by Gulf sovereign funds, Indian and Russian oligarchs. While oligarchs invest on their own account, the SWF is presumably doing so on behalf of Qatar's population. "The vast gas-rich state of Qatar has invested much of its vast wealth in the UK", *The Guardian* reported in November 2022,[12] "It has more than £40 billions of British assets, including stakes in Barclays Bank, Sainsbury's, Heathrow, and British Airways". Now, I have no problems with the Qataris owning prize stakes in listed British companies like Barclays or British Airways. The investment terms are disclosed and so are the rates of return.

When it comes to London property acquisitions by the QIA or by individual members of the ruling family, it becomes difficult to ascertain whether the purchase is for vanity reasons or to drive genuine rates of return. The first problem is the sheer volume of the transactions. Here is *The Guardian* once again:

- The Ritz, Claridge's, the Savoy, the Connaught, the Berkeley, the Churchill, Grosvenor House, and the Intercontinental Park Plane – worth more than £5 billion by some estimated – are wholly or partly Qatari-owned.
- Upmarket retail has proved irresistible too. Qatar bought Harrods in 2010 for about £1.5 billion. The former emir also owns luxury brands Valentino, Balmain, and Pal Zileri, including their salubrious London outlets.
- Qatar dominates the skyline too. Its SWF paid £1.1 billion for HSBC's HQ in 2014, then led a takeover of Canary Wharf Group, which owns the financial hub in London's Docklands.
- No asset symbolises Qatar's financial muscle more than The Shard. The emirate financed the £2 billion development and owns land around the imposing 310-m tower too, including the News Building occupied by Rupert Murdoch's News UK.

To top it all, the Qataris are significant landowners in the UK, "owning nearly 2.1 million square metres (23 million square feet) of property in Britain, more than 1.5 times the area of London's Hyde Park". Readers may object to my characterisation of the Qatari investments in London and the UK, my home city and country, as representing vanity showpieces. I say this because it is questionable what rates of return these property investments are yielding to the QIA and other entities. In the aftermath of Brexit and the pandemic, the London property market has been buffeted by a serious economic slowdown which has impacted investor enthusiasm. Even at the best of times, it is not easy for any land or property owner in London to sell trophy assets like The Shard or Harrods. Should property prices stagnate or at worse plummet, these will prove to be stranded investments for the owners. The objective of any SWF, as highlighted at the start of the chapter, is to invest for the long term and to serve as a rainy day fund. In the case of Qatar, this is for the day when natural gas reserves eventually run out and/or are supplanted by green energy alternatives. That day may well be decades away, but it does beg the question whether the country's ruling class is wisely investing for the future.

A similar comment can be made about Saudi Arabia's giant Public Investment Fund (PIF) (assets $1.1 trillion) which went on a binge acquiring trophy sporting assets all over the world. This includes the English Premier League team Newcastle United, the launch of a new challenger league to the PGA through LIV Golf, sponsorship of the International Cricket Council, and in horse racing. "Although other nation-states have exerted influence on global sport, we have never seen anything as comprehensive as Saudi Arabia's vast investments in a multitude of different sports over the past few years", reported *The Athletic.*[13] Saudi Arabia is also the host for the 2034 World Cup Soccer tournament so the push into world sports probably makes sense, particularly given recent soaring valuations of sports franchises. With a population of 37 million, Saudi is also in a dramatically different (and difficult) economic context compared with Qatar (population 3.07 million). The prospect of oil demand running out soon is making Saudi policymakers extremely nervous. The kingdom's population skews young, and the economy needs to generate millions of quality jobs in the non-oil sector. Which explains why the PIF appears to be reconfiguring its approach more recently by placing a greater emphasis on investing at home.

At the annual Future Investment Initiative (FII) held each October since 2017 in Riyadh (described by media as "Davos in the desert"), investment bankers and global companies seeking investment have eagerly participated to get access to Saudi petrodollars and lucrative deal fees. These deals are likely to taper off as Saudi authorities wisely turn their attention inwards and attempt to boost domestic investment and demand, as the recent annual report of the PIF shows. "The PIF's report marks a shift from externally driven investments to a focus on domestic opportunities. The days of viewing Saudi Arabia as a mere financial reservoir are ending", one FII participant told *CNBC.*[14]

Which brings us to the good i.e. SWFs and other investors from the emerged world who are expanding their investment footprint eastwards and are doing it with clear, strategic investment goals in mind. Before we jump into these examples, it is important to lay out a few principles which make good SWFs in emerged markets stand out from the rest.

- **Principle 1:** The wealth fund or sovereign (i.e. China) should have a clear purpose, investment thesis, and objectives. Becoming the largest landowner in London might seem to be a splendid objective until one compare investment return from other assets and markets.
- **Principle 2:** Not every fund can aspire to be like the Norwegians, who have set a high bar in terms of transparency and disclosure. But there should be a level of transparency and disclosure in emerged market sovereigns which the citizen from the source country can relate to.
- **Principle 3:** The governance of wealth funds or sovereign should be beyond reproach. While it is important to have senior leaders or the ruler to head the wealth fund, there should be a clearly explainable organisation structure on how decisions are taken and risks considered and mitigated.
- **Principle 4:** The concept of stewardship, which in simple terms means that the monies being managed by the wealth funds are being managed responsibly on behalf of the citizens of the country, should be clearly articulated.

Taking these four principles into consideration, the wealth funds of Singapore and the UAE clearly stand out as good examples of capital management and focus on returns. I hasten to add that they are by no means perfect, addressing critics who are likely to pillory me for praising them. I have been an interested observer in these funds for several years – based in Singapore and Dubai – and can assert with a great deal of confidence that these SWFs do stand out from the rest of the pack. Let's test each of the principles to see if the Singapore SWF – GIC – and the UAE counterparts (ADIA and Mubadala notably), partially or fully live up to these standards. In terms of Principle 1 – articulating purpose and a clear, underlying investment thesis – GIC and ADIA, Mubadala are standouts. GIC, for example, articulates its common purpose as being "securing Singapore's financial future". Mubadala notes that its mandate "is to generate sustainable long-term returns within acceptable risk parameters to our Shareholder, while delivering positive impact on current and future generations".

Some might quibble that this is purple prose, the usual corporate rhetoric which cannot be validated and backed up by hard data. They do have a point because both GIC and Mubadala fall short of Principle 2 – transparency and disclosure. As noted earlier, GIC does not disclose the total size of its investment portfolio but only the rates of return it has generated on its portfolio. Mubadala fares slightly better by disclosing both the rate of return and assets under management. However, we know very little about the SWF's actual annual financial performance, noting that such information is "irrelevant" to the long-term investor. Using the Norwegian SWF as a benchmark, both GIC and Mubadala appear to be dancing in the dark when it comes to disclosing the positives and negatives in their vast global portfolios.

However, the test is in Principle 3 – whether there is a high degree of public confidence in the governance of these SWFs. In Singapore, while there is some public discussion on the full extent of GIC's assets, the fact that the SWF has a clear governance structure, with the Prime Minister at the top of the pyramid and a professional management team fulfilling a public mandate to secure Singapore's financial future, has built accountability and confidence in the system. Mubadala has also significantly increased its disclosure and has UAE's Vice President serving as Chair with other local luminaries on the Board. The strong governance structure allows for better communications about accountability and public trust (Principle 4), which are critical as SWFs navigate an increasingly volatile global context. Nobody expects the SWFs to operate risk-free or mistake-free in their investment approach. The very nature of investing for the future entails responsible risk-taking and an ability to disclose and come clean when mistakes do occur. This is the true definition of investment stewardship.

The risks are likely to magnify as the US-China strategic competition accelerates, and some SWFs have already been caught up in the newish variant of the Cold War. When I was growing up in India, the unholy troika of state subsidies, industrial policy, and privileging local business over foreign rivals were often described as reasons for the country's anaemic growth performance. In terms of economic ideology, we appear to have come full circle with American and Europe, harsh critics of the India and developing country policies illustrated above, have enthusiastically pursued similar policies. Former US National Security Advisor Jake Sullivan articulated the Biden administration's aggressive industrial policy objective as "building a small yard with a tall fence".[15] In his tenure, Sullivan was forthright in defending America's right to protect its intellectual property. "Chokepoints for foundational technologies have to be inside the yard and the fence has to be high – because our strategic competitors should not be able to exploit American and allied technologies to undermine American and allied security", Sullivan said in a speech in October 2022.

While Sullivan left open the possibility of partnering with allies and friendly nations, this radical shift in American policy is directly impacting the investment prospects of the SWFs. For example, Mubadala's plans to acquire America's Fortress Investment Group in 2023 hit regulatory hurdles, specifically from the powerful Committee on Foreign Investment in the United States (CFIUS), the US Treasury committee responsible for screening inbound and outbound investment in strategic sectors, the definition of which has been expanded significantly to include almost every sector where China has an edge. The deal was eventually cleared, quite possibly because of the UAE's warm ties with America but it illustrates that SWFs, even from friendly nations, must navigate greater US regulatory scrutiny. Researcher Udaibir Das, a former IMF colleague, has written[16] that a "trio" of three unconnected phenomena – fragmentation, uncertainty, and geopolitics – is significantly reshaping the FDI landscape.

> The trio of risks is gradually forcing state-owned funds to reconsider their investment outlook. This is a shift from the past, where they relied solely on traditional asset allocation models, which are primarily driven by inflation, interest rates, and growth considerations.

He adds that the fragmented global landscape presents significant challenges for allocating state-owned investable capital. "But by adopting innovative strategies, diversifying investments, and fostering partnerships, state-owned funds can navigate these complexities and continue to play a vital role in global economic growth and development".

Diversification is being forced on the SWFs as they seek investment in friendlier shores to the east and the south. However, they need to learn new lessons in how their investments are likely to transform economic development outcomes in emerged countries so that mistakes from investing in the west can be avoided. While evidence of deglobalisation is patchy, the great investment wave of the 21st century may well be in the emerged world. A group of countries as illustrated in this chapter have accumulated savings which were unimaginable even two decades ago. The capital they are prepared to deploy should give them a greater say in how the world economy is run and multilateral institutions managed. They should also not be victimised for using the reserve currency *du jour,* the dollar. On these fundamental platform and governance issues, as we will discover in the next chapter, the current status quo is terribly unequal.

Notes

1 Speech at Temasek's 30th Anniversary Dinner, November 2, 2004.
2 This estimate is from the Sovereign Wealth Fund Institute.
3 Essay by Lim Chow Kiat – GIC's Long-Term View, March 17, 2015.
4 Data is from the Global SWF data platform – www.globalswf.com.
5 World Bank Blogs, December 18, 2024 – Dilip Ratha et al.
6 This is of course not the precise translation of Deng's quote, which he is believed to have adapted from an ancient Chinese proverb.
7 The Belt and Road Initiative: A Key Pillar of the Global Community of Shared Future – published by the State Council Information Office, October 2023.
8 Larry Summers on X, April 14, 2023.
9 The 2008 Housing Crisis – Don't Blame Federal Housing Programs for Wall Street's Recklessness – CAP Report, April 13, 2017.

10 Debunking the myth of "debt trap diplomacy" – Research paper published by Chatham House, December 14, 2020.
11 China and private lenders are blocking a solution to the global debt crisis. The G20 must step in – Vasuki Shastry and Jeremy Mark, Atlantic Council, February 22, 2023.
12 All data and information cited above is from *The Guardian* – How Qatar bought up Britain – November 5, 2022.
13 Saudi Arabia's takeover of world sport – The Athletic, February 2, 2024.
14 No longer a financial reservoir – CNBC, August 23, 2024.
15 Like every idea or concept in DC, the phrase originated in a think-tank and was widely embraced by the Biden administration to describe its industrial policy approach to counter China.
16 The trio of risks reshaping SWF strategies – Udaibir Das, fDi Intelligence, October/November 2024.

Chapter 4

Platforms

Emerged markets have a greater weight in the global economy, but they are still playing second fiddle to the G7.

I would like to start with an apology and a joke in that order. I would like to apologise to anyone who may be offended by the joke, told to me by an Asian policymaker many years ago. The objective is to illuminate the inequities faced by emerged markets rather than to cause insult or injury. So, taking a deep breath, here goes. It is now well known that the Ten Commandments were revealed to Moses on Mount Sinai, as described in Exodus. The Asian policymaker, with a wink in his eye, assured me that after receiving the Ten Commandments, Moses was recalled to Mount Sinai to receive an additional Two Commandments. Without further ado, this is what Moses received as Commandments 11 and 12:

> There shall be a rules-based international order, hereinafter to be referred to as RBIO, as set by the leading powers of the day and shalt be followed by all, irrespective of their inequities.
>
> The Managing Director of the IMF shalt always be European, and the President of the World Bank shalt always be American, even if there are other capable candidates.
>
> So let it be written, let it be done (this last bit is not from God or Moses but from the Cecil B de Mille movie!).

Yes, this is a joke, and the Asian policymaker guffawed loudly after relating it at a dinner. As a joke, it is also a cruel one as many emerged market policymakers will attest. Almost eight decades after the end of World War II, when global powers of the day carved up how the world should be governed, we are still living in a system created in that era and which is hopelessly out of date. Despite the many injuries and deaths, it suffered because of World War I and II, the UK was still a leading global power

DOI: 10.4324/9781003603375-6

at the end of 1945. It had not given up its colonies, and India remained a jewel in its crown. Today, that very colonial subject has outpaced the UK in terms of GDP and outranked it in the global economy's pecking order. In 1945, it was entirely appropriate therefore for the UK, along with other victors America, France, and the USSR, to dictate how the world should be run and wrote the rules to support their projection of power. There was of course an immediate decoupling as the USSR and America were soon at odds, triggering a decades long Cold War. This allowed the Western powers, led by America and soon joined by other members of the G7 (the UK, France, Germany, Canada, Italy, and to a more limited extent Japan) to frame the global rules of the road.

Here is former US Secretary of State Anthony Blinken[1] describing the RBIO to a new generation.

> We must defend and reform the rules-based international order, the system of laws, agreements, principles, and institutions that the world came together to build after two world wars to manage relations between states, to prevent conflict, to uphold the rights of all people. Its founding documents include the UN Charter and the Universal Declaration of Human Rights, which enshrines concepts like self-determination, sovereignty, the peaceful settlement of disputes. These are not western constructs. They are the reflection of the world's shared aspirations.

Now, there is nothing objectionable in Blinken's comments with two important caveats. There is overwhelming empirical evidence to support the proposition that the RBIO, in economic but not all other aspects, did deliver unprecedented economic prosperity (particularly during the glory growth years of Europe, circa 1945 through 1975, and in America for much longer after), allowing for the dramatic expansion in trade and investment worldwide. The multilateral institutions which were created from the rubble of World War II – the United Nations and allied agencies, the IMF, the World Bank, and eventually the WTO – created the foundations for a norms-based and rules-based order which we should all be grateful for. But as Paul Gewirtz notes, we should not "romanticise" the RBIO.

> It has failed to prevent many kinetic wars, the Cold War, economic crises, and human rights disasters. Even after the Cold War ended and the United States became the "hegemonic" global leader, the international system hardly stopped crisis from emerging throughout the world,

he writes.[2]

The caveats I offer therefore are two-fold. The RBIO, as it is written and practised today, differentiates between the rule-makers (America, supported by Europe) and the rule-takers (rest of the world). There is a clear subservient relationship which the rule-takers are expected to follow and comply with the rules set by the rule-makers. The second caveat is the refusal on the part of the rule-makers that the world has fundamentally changed since 1945. Not only have economic weights of the emerged world dramatically increased, particularly with the rise of China and India, they are rightly demanding equal voice and representation in *how* global rules are originated and shaped. To use a crude example, if RBIO is a children's playground, the leading powers are behaving like petulant children refusing to share toys with the new kids on the block, who have gained and prospered in recent years. This has created an unhealthy situation where the leading powers routinely invoke the RBIO as the reason why the developing world should support a specific policy or position (Russia's invasion of Ukraine is a classic example), without acknowledging that the rule-takers should have agency and an independent voice in determining what is best for their own national interests. This explains why Indian Foreign Minister went on a tirade against Europe, which I described in a previous chapter, and the fact that RBIO lecturing by the west no longer falls on receptive ears. There is also an attempt underway to frame the debate on a rules-based order as being part of the great contest between America and China. This, in my view, offers a free pass to the rule-makers not to reform the global order at all, on spurious grounds that they don't want to concede ground to a rising power.

There is genuine contestation between America and China for global supremacy today, which cannot be denied. As early as 2017, Chinese President Xi Jinping was warning[3] about "inadequate economic governance", which was making it difficult for the global economy to adjust to new developments. "The global economic landscape has changed profoundly in the past few decades. However, the global governance has not embraced those new changes and is therefore inadequate in terms of representation and inclusiveness". I was at Davos that January when Xi delivered his speech. It appeared to be an inflection point for the global economy, with President Trump about to assume power in a few days, a moment which was then regarded as America's pull-back from the very system it had created and nurtured for decades. China stood out as a staunch defender of globalisation, and the RBIO of course interpreted very differently in Beijing compared with Blinken's definition earlier in the chapter.

Even before Trump came into office, China and a group of emerging markets were complaining about the lack of meaningful governance reforms at economic institutions like the IMF and the World Bank. They had two major complaints. First, shareholding in the IMF which is determined by the economic weight of a country is still heavily skewed in favour of America and Europe. Under an idealistic RBIO mechanism, if implemented in full, China's share at the IMF would substantially increase from current levels of 6%, posing a challenge to America's supreme position as the largest shareholder (around 17%), with an effective veto since major decisions at the Fund require the support of 85% of the membership. In lockstep, the shareholding weights of other emerged market countries like India, Brazil, and South Africa would also see a concomitant increase, transforming the league table of the top ten powerful shareholder of the institution. In a piece I wrote for *Forbes*,[4] which led to some trolling on X, I had argued that Europe had a disproportionately greater say in running the IMF.

> How can one explain that Korea with a GDP of $1.8 trillion has a lower share of votes at the IMF than t he Netherlands (GDP of 1 trillion). How can one defend tiny Belgium (GDP $595 billion) having a significantly higher share compared with Indonesia (GDP $1.1 trillion). Even so, as Europeans well know, the combined voting strength of China, India, Indonesia, Japan, and Korea today exceeds the weight of major European nations.

Brazil's former representative at the IMF Board, Paulo Nogueira Batista, argues in a working paper[5] that the rivalry between the West, led by the US, and emerging powers, notably China is at the root of the current widespread pessimism concerning IMF reforms.

> Always a difficult endeavour, this reform now stumbles on the fact the main shareholders, the United States, European countries, and Japan, as well as other high-income nations, are dead set against contemplating any reform that would provide more decision-making power for China.

He adds that China, however, is precisely the country that is "most heavily underrepresented" by any conceivable metric, and, therefore, the one that most stands to gain from a redistribution of quotas and voting power in the IMF. Batista recommends that emerging and developing countries (EMDCs in his definition) should not "abandon" the IMF, precisely because of its centrality in the global economic system, but pursue a "gradualist" approach for pursuing shareholding reforms.

For me personally, this is a difficult point to accept because of the second reason why emerged countries are so upset with the governance of the IMF and the World Bank – "the 12th commandment" which dictates that an American will always head the World Bank and a European would be at the helm of the IMF. I worked for the IMF for 17+ years and served under five Managing Directors, all European. Barring one, whom I shall not name, all of them were outstanding economists and technocrats, having served in senior positions in government at home. During the same period, the World Bank saw leadership transition four times, all American and again barring one were at the top of their game.

The crucial point here is that during the same period, the emerged world also had their best and brightest serving in economic leadership positions at home, who, at a moment's notice, were fully capable as serving as the heads of the IMF and the World Bank. On this list of contenders, I would include Singapore's Tharman Shanmugaratnam, India's Montek Singh Ahluwalia, Brazil's Arminio Fraga, Mexico's Agustin Carstens, China's Min Zhu, Indonesia's Sri Mulyani Indrawati, and South Africa's Tito Mboweni. Many critics and trolls have pointed out that the above candidates may well have succeeded had emerged nations sufficiently united behind a single candidate. For example, Agustin Carstens contested the 2012 IMF Managing Director race, which was settled in favour of Christine Lagarde, because Brazil and other nations refused to support the Mexican's candidacy (over-reported concerns that Carstens was "too much" of a "Chicago boy", a reference to his education at the University of Chicago and therefore commitment to economic orthodoxy). There will always be differences between emerged nations on economic and political ideology but a rules-based order which does away with the convention of only having an American and European running two of the most important multilateral economic institutions will see a proliferation of capable and electable candidates. Despite its many flaws, the selection process for the top job at the UN system is via regional rotation, at least ensuring that geographically diverse candidates have a shot at securing the Secretary General job at the UN.

Reading this paragraph, American and European officials, while not denying the capabilities of the above candidates, will privately say that the two leading multilateral institutions should be headed by "creditor nations" i.e. countries which provide the most capital to the two institutions and happen to be major aid donors. The donor issue can easily be addressed with China's emergence as a profligate aid provider, often surpassing absolute levels of assistance provided by the OECD grouping. Other emerged countries – India and Brazil notably – have also stepped-up development assistance. The definition of a "creditor nation", which in the old days only meant America and Europe, is thoroughly outdated as China, India, and Brazil are fully capable of meeting their due share of IMF, World Bank capital requirements, and in stepping up bilateral aid.

I would like to differentiate between China's response to the governance abnormalities – which in short order led to the creation of two multilateral institutions under China's orbit, the Asian Infrastructure Investment Bank (AIIB) and the New Development Bank (NDB), both headquartered in China – and the rest of the emerged world. To use the buffet metaphor highlighted in an earlier chapter, countries like India (which is involved in a serious border conflict with China), Brazil, and Indonesia don't see a contradiction in being members of the AIIB and simultaneously with the World Bank and the IMF. They want access to finance, wherever it is provided, and don't want to make geopolitical judgements by aligning their foreign policy with such access. This pragmatism flies in the face of the current world disorder, where fragmentation of trade, investment, and technological flows are the norm.

Professor Danny Quah of Singapore's Lee Kuan Yew School of Public Policy writes[6] that the "parameters" of the challenge of global fragmentation make urgent the need for some mechanism that can help check the destabilising dynamics that are already in place. Quah's first principle is to use a nations' self-interests: "look for problem domains where *inadvertent cooperation* arises i.e., where nations even though only looking out for just their self-interest end up, inadvertently, improving the collective good". Under his formulation, "inadvertent cooperation occurs when collective well-being rises even though there is no conscious attempt at collaboration". His second formulation to preserve some semblance of world order is for nations to "divide and conquer" between inadvertent cooperation, zero-sum problems, and what he defines as epic fail features. "Under certain conditions, epic fail problems offer the possibility of third-party nudges i.e. small side payments, judiciously applied, can produce a large shift in the equilibrium outcome, away from where everyone loses to where everyone wins". A third, even more controversial proposal from Quah concerns the future durability of multilateralism in preserving the world order. He proposes a "constrained multilateralism", a plurilateral system where all features of multilateralism apply but membership is strictly restricted to a "subset of the entire community of nations". "All nations are free to join or leave a plurilateral system, but the requirement is that those within must obey its rules while those outside are not permitted to disrupt", he writes

> By remaining open and inclusive in potential membership while requiring certain codes of behaviour for those inside, a plurilateral system can be effective in delivering a restricted multilateralism and, additionally, can permit full-blown multilateralism to re-emerge when the larger community see benefits for all.

I want to put Quah's research hypothesis to test by examining the BRICS grouping. Now, I am assuming that everyone has heard or read about the BRICS, which started as an investment proposition conceived by Goldman Sachs economists over two decades ago. The initial BRIC coinage only included Brazil, Russia, India, and China, but creative political commentators soon included South Africa into the list and started advocating for greater policy coordination on global issues. This germ of an idea morphed into a ministerial process, at finance and foreign minister level, which has since been upgraded to include an annual meeting of heads of state. In a fracturing world, the BRICS grouping hopes to gain more political heft by including several new members – Egypt, Ethiopia, Indonesia, Iran, the UAE notably – and two of its original members, Russia and China, clearly regard the expanded BRICS+ as a bulwark against the Western-dominated multilateral system.

Jim O'Neill, the Goldman Sachs economist who coined the BRIC phrase, is now deeply sceptical about the expansion of the grouping and its political aspirations. "The fact is that truly global challenges cannot be addressed through narrow groupings like the BRICS (or the G7 for that matter), and this will remain the case no matter how many members they add", he wrote recently "What we really need is a rejuvenated G20, which proved highly effective in its earliest days, following the 2008 financial crisis".[7] While I agree with O'Neill that a truly multilateral grouping such as the G20 can be more effective on the world stage, I don't share his cynicism that the BRICS don't matter (which was the headline of the piece outlined above). The proliferation of regional groupings such as BRICS+ is precisely because the existing system is regarded by many developing countries as being patently unfair. The BRICS head of state summit, held in Kazan, Russia, in October 2024, reflected many of the scepticism expressed by O'Neill but some hopeful signs as well.

With 24 heads of state/governments in attendance, including representatives from non-BRICs nations (Sri Lanka, Indonesia's new foreign minister), the BRICS summit was an impressive gathering of rising and middle powers. While Western commentators dismissed the summit for lacking substance, long-time BRICS watchers have noted that the growing number of countries participating in the summit (and wishing to formally join) is a clear sign that developing countries regard it as an important platform to engage. For the G7, it was a galling sight as Russian President Putin effortlessly presided over the proceedings as though there was no war against neighbouring Ukraine. The fundamental question must be asked as to why so many emerged countries felt comfortable attending the summit despite being uncomfortable with Russia's brazen infringement of national sovereignty in Ukraine. In my view, it was their deep unhappiness with the existing status quo, where they are passive rule-takers rather than collaborative rule-makers.

The Kazan communique, as to be expected, was full of the usual platitudes on conflict resolution (Ukraine, Gaza, Lebanon) but the most notable intervention at the summit came from India. It is obvious that Russia and China regard the BRICS grouping as primarily being *anti-Western* in its approach. Indian officials laid out clear red lines in their official interactions:

- **India's vision for BRICS:** A diverse and inclusive platform. An organisation willing to evolve over time. Giving our own example to the world we must collectively and in a united manner, raise our voice for reform of global institutions.

- **Caution about BRICS becoming an anti-west platform:** Indian officials emphasised that BRICS is a "non-west" rather than an anti-west platform. The approach must remain "people centric" and convey the message that the organisation is not divisive and is working for in the interest of humanity. "***We must be careful to ensure that the organisation does not acquire the image of one that is trying to replace global institutions, instead of being perceived as one that wishes to reform them***". *(itals mine)*

India, unlike Russia and China, does not see the UN, the IMF, and World Bank as being antithetical to the new order which the BRICS grouping wishes to usher in. This position is likely to increasingly place it at odds against Russia, China, Iran, and others, implying that the BRICS can never aspire to be the kind of plurilateral multilateralism which Quah has in mind. It is because of these inherent contradictions which prompted many commentators, including O'Neill, to be dismissive about the durability of BRICS+. India's position reflects both a commitment to improve and strengthen the existing multilateral system while agitating from the outside with groupings such as BRICS+ for reform and change. To be sure, there are plenty of commonsensical economic areas where the BRICS+ can collaborate, short of supplanting the existing order. The Kazan meeting, for example, also yielded modest progress on economic and trade issues, mainly regarded as Russia-driven initiatives. They include plans to establish a BRICS Grain Exchange, the use of local currencies in establishing a cross-border payment system, and an "independent" cross-border settlement and depository infrastructure. Thankfully, the BRICS proposal to establish a common currency was swiftly put to bed by India and other prominent members. At a time of severe sanctions placed on it by the G7, Russia would undoubtedly prefer not having the US dollar as *the* global reserve currency. China, on its part, flirted with the idea of positioning its own currency as a potential alternative to the dollar many years ago but Beijing has backed away from that plan since then.

To understand why so many countries resent having the dollar as the dominant reserve currency (and simultaneously can't live without it), one must first understand the "exorbitant privilege"[8] bestowed upon the US for having the dollar as the only currency in town. It enables the US government to borrow dollars, in theory without any limit, and its financial system immensely benefitting from the simple fact that an overwhelming portion of global trade (54% of export invoicing) and share of foreign exchange transactions touching the dollar (88%) takes place in the greenback.

If the global economy can be described as the human body, the dollar is the vital arteries which pumps blood to the heart and the brain. In a conversation in Brussels many years ago, an EU official expressed frustration that the US government was "weaponising" the dollar by imposing sanctions and fines against European financial institutions for minor and major infractions. I was at the meeting with a senior bank colleague, who skilfully explained that the primacy of the dollar meant that US authorities not only had the power to check alleged abuse of the system but also had access to the raw data and the intelligence to understand real-time developments in the global economy. The dollar, under his construct, was both a reserve currency and a major data gathering platform, not very different from the business models of American social media firms such as Google or Meta. How does this happen in practice? If you are a major international bank with the coveted dollar clearing license, this allows you to accept deposits in the currency and vitally to provide loans and other services to clients globally. Conversely, central banks of foreign governments also keep their precious foreign reserves in dollars, often placing the surplus in US Treasuries. The Atlantic Council estimates that the dollar represents around 58% of the value of foreign reserve holdings worldwide. The euro takes second place, with only 20% of foreign reserve holdings. Every touchpoint in this complex dollar-based system involves reporting and regulatory requirements to various branches of the US government, sometimes onerous and punitive, if breached.

The exorbitant privilege is therefore both a blessing (which explains why the dollar is still regarded as the ultimate safe haven asset by emerged countries at times of crisis) and a curse (institutions or individuals found crossing the line face the risk of being fined or jailed). The US also has the power to essentially cut away a country from the dollar-based system, as happened with Russia in the aftermath of its invasion of Ukraine. This was a serious wake-up call for China, which has parked an estimated $758 billion of its foreign reserves in US Treasuries which could potentially be blocked should it decide to invade Taiwan. China, as Russia has, could also lose access to the dollar-based SWIFT settlement system. "BRICS members have turned their attention away from a shared currency and towards new cross-border systems with the goal of creating a more multipolar financial system", The Atlantic Council notes, in its appropriately titled "Dollar Dominance Monitor",[9] "China has led this effort by accelerating its development of the Cross-Border Interbank Payment System (CIPS) – a renminbi settlement mechanism". Between June 2023 and May 2024, CIPS added 62 direct participants and now comprises 142 direct and 1,394 indirect participants, quite a contrast with SWIFT's 11,000 connected banks.

There are few issues within emerged markets which agitate and excite economic policymakers as much as the primacy of the dollar and why it needs to be replaced. Central banks, even those from developed countries, fume at what they regard as excessive and hubristic actions by various arms of the US government by imposing sanctions, which depending on the gravity of the case prevents entire nations, specific companies and individuals, from access to the system. The fines imposed by US regulators against financial institutions also touched eye-popping levels in the past decade. Exhibit A – the $8.9 billion paid by French bank BNP Paribas in 2015 – is a standout example. I am not excusing the alleged crimes committed by the bank here. It was accused of wilfully violating sanctions against doing business with Iran, Sudan, and Cuba by providing alternative and illegal channels for Iranian entities to access the dollar system. Daleep Singh, who served as former President Biden's deputy national security advisor, was one of the architects of the sanctions imposed against Russia in 2022. He acknowledges[10] that during this short century, major powers have deployed economic sanctions and other restrictive tools of what he describes as "economic statecraft" to an unprecedented degree. "The number of sanctioned individuals and entities across the world has increased by an order of magnitude since 2000", he noted. Other examples include the introduction of tariffs and trade restrictions, which have tripled over the last five years and even turbocharged by the second Trump administration.

> The percentage of OECD countries screening investments in sensitive sectors has risen over the past decade from less than a third to over 80 percent, while the number of countries with sophisticated export controls has quadrupled since their inception since the Cold War,

he added, noting that this phenomenon was global, including similar restrictions introduced by China.

At the same time, US regulators are behaving like a man with the veritable hammer – they see nails everywhere to be hammered. If used diligently, the threat of sanctions will genuinely protect the integrity of the system. It is the excessive use of sanctions and fines which has cast America as the arch villain in many emerged parts of the world. Policymakers, notably Brazilian President Lula, want the dollar to be replaced *manana* and pronto but the sober reality is that a serious competitor is nowhere in sight. In 2009, the US Treasury identified six criteria[11] which enables a country to issue and dominate a reserve currency. The criteria include the following parameters and my assessment below on whether China meets the threshold:

- A sizeable domestic economy – Yes, for China
- Importance of the economy in international trade – Yes, for China
- Size, depth, openness of the financial markets – Not yet, for China

- Convertibility of the currency – No, for China
- Use of the currency as a currency peg or anchor currency – No, for China
- Stable domestic macroeconomic conditions and policies – Maybe, for China.

While my assessment is subjective, it still shows that China is well short of widely accepted criteria for any currency to achieve reserve currency status. This is not a college admission exam where China could perhaps study harder and improve its scoring over a period of time. The principal reason why China falls short in positioning the renminbi as a global reserve currency is because it has actively chosen not to either make the currency fully convertible or allow other countries who trade with it to peg their own currencies with the renminbi. There are various complicated reasons why China still prefers to retain a command-and-control approach over this currency and the economy at large. Writing in October 2020,[12] my former IMF colleague Eswar Prasad said that there is a question of whether the renminbi could realistically aspire to the status of a "safe haven" currency. Such a currency, in his view, is the one that investors turn to for safety during times of global turmoil. History suggests, he added, that country seeking this status must have a sound institutional framework, including an independent judiciary, an open and transparent government with institutionalised checks and balances, and robust public institutions (especially a credible central bank).

> In short, while the renminbi has the potential to become a significant reserve currency, it is unlikely to attain safe haven status in the absence of far-reaching reforms to China's institutional and political structures. Under the present regime, the prospects of such changes are dim.

The emerged world must make a strategic choice. Tilt at the windmills and rage and rant about the primacy of the dollar, which will yield limited results. It is entirely appropriate for countries at the receiving end of America's extra-territorial action to push back and demand fair application of the rules. I live in D.C. most of the year and familiar with the internal policy debates about the wisdom of the continued weaponisation of the dollar. They are the power hawks, who believe that it is legitimate for a hegemonic power to deploy economic warfare to demand compliance from a pliant world. D.C. also has its fair share of power doves from both sides of the political aisle who believe that the man with a hammer approach to impose sanctions and block access will eventually force the world to seek alternative modes of currency and payment systems. The recent gold rush which saw the value of the precious metal surge 23%

in 2023 and an additional 28% in 2024 is a sign that central banks and ordinary investors are seeking alternative store of value options away from the greenback. This includes crypto assets. However, talk of the so-called "dollar debasement" trade is clearly overblown because of the obvious limitations of gold and crypto assets.

The emerged world should build a coalition with the power doves to ensure that there are guardrails to America's economic warfare. Author and former journalist Paul Blustein says that when it comes to managing dollar supremacy, US authorities should be guided by the adage of Marvel comic superhero *Spiderman* – "with great power comes great responsibility". "No other economy can rival America's capacity to generate safe and liquid assets", he writes[13] "But US complacency about the dollar's role – or worse, imperiousness – would be seriously misguided".

There is a serious policy debate within the US on the domestic costs of the dollar being the world's reserve currency. Serious misgivings too about the status quo, where America's rising debt and budget deficits are funded by countries like China. Economist Michael Pettis, somewhat provocatively, has written[14] that global economic imbalances are "real" i.e. China generating persistent and abnormal trade surpluses and the US generating deficits on the other side of the trade balance sheet. His solution is the formation of a customs union (along the lines proposed by economist John Maynard Keynes, when the IMF and the World Bank were established), where "countries must recognise the external consequences of their policies and must take steps to keep domestic demand and domestic supply in overall balance". However, if the world is unable to reach such an agreement, Pettis says that the US is "justified" to act unilaterally to "reverse" its role in accommodating policy distortions abroad, as it is doing now. "The most effective way is likely to be by imposing controls on the US capital account that limit the ability of surplus countries to balance their surpluses by acquiring US assets".

An even more radical proposal originated from Stephen Miran, currently in the powerful position of Chairman of President Trump's Council of Economic Advisors (and temporary appointee to the Federal Reserve). In a paper issued[15] after Trump's election victory in November 2024, Miran called for a "Mar A Lago" accord between America and major trading nations which run a trade surplus against the country. In effect, and I am simplifying here, Miran called on these nations to collectively take steps to weaken the dollar (by selling a portion of their reserves) and simultaneously agree to increase the duration of their holdings of US Treasuries, in effect submitting to a reduction in the face value of their holdings. To put it simply and bluntly, any unilateral moves by the US to force investment losses on US Treasury holdings held by other countries would have a catastrophic impact on bond markets, the value of the dollar, and in turn the global economy. It would be an own goal for the US economy and accelerate the demise of the dollar as a reserve currency.

Emerged countries have a common interest in pushing back against these radical proposals. They should also pursue a nuanced approach to reform the RBIO from within and to apply pressure on a global system which appears to be suffering from amnesia about the real shifts in balance of power. The classical definition of balance of power, which originated in the 16th century, posits that peace is the outcome when any one state, faction, or figure is prevented from gaining enough power to dominate all others. The anomaly now is that in geopolitics, there is a fierce contest between an incumbent power and a rising one to alter that balance of power. In the economic sphere, the focus of this book, power is more evenly balanced between the status quo powers and a group of rising nations. It is possible to achieve appropriate balance, voice, and representation in the multilateral system so that all powers can collaborate and feel they have a genuine stake. The alternative of course is multilateral decoupling, with potentially catastrophic outcomes for the global economy. The world is bereft of ideas, the focus of our next chapter, which should be the reason alone to push for innovative reforms which will protect the existing order (by rebalancing power equations), rather than attempting to build a new, messier alternative.

Notes

1 The Blinken quote was cited in the *Financial Times*, The Rachman Review, April 20, 2023.
2 China, the US, and the future of a rules-based international order – Paul Gewirtz, Brookings Institution, July 22, 2024.
3 President Xi Jinping – Speech at World Economic Forum annual meeting, Davos, January 17, 2017.
4 As IMF's Georgieva Seeks a New Term, Why Asia Should Call Out Europe – Forbes Asia, March 14, 2024.
5 A way out for IMF reform – Paulo Nogueira Batista, Bretton Woods Project, June 2024.
6 Forthcoming paper by Danny Quah – Economic Principles for a New World Order of Multipolarity and Multilateralism – April 2024.
7 The BRICS still don't matter – Jim O'Neill, Project Syndicate, October 17, 2024.
8 The phrase was originally used by the late French politician Valery Giscard d" Estaing.
9 Dollar Dominance Monitor, Atlantic Council.
10 Daleep Singh – speech at Atlantic Council, January 16, 2025.
11 US Treasury, Report to Congress on International Economic and Exchange Rate Policies – October 2009.
12 The renminbi rises but will not rival the dollar – Eswar Prasad, Brookings Institution, October 2020.

13 Dollar's primacy and the web of global responsibilities – Paul Blustein, Financial Times, August 1, 2023.
14 America would be better off without the global dollar – Michael Pettis, Financial Times, 16 April 2025.
15 A User's Guide to Restructuring the Global Trading System – Stephen Miran, Hudson Bay Capital, November 2024.

Chapter 5

Ideas

America was the greatest idea and ideal of the 20th century. As it commits self-harm, other more compelling ideas are gaining momentum.

In May 2020, as the pandemic surged around the world, an American journalist Megan Stack, based in Singapore, wrote a seemingly innocuous column for *The New York Times*. Titled "A Sudden Coronavirus Surge Brought Out Singapore's Dark Side",[1] Stack wrote about the divides in the city-state, between wealthy, settled Singaporeans (who were well protected from the pandemic) and the foreign worker class, where the virus had spread across dormitories where they were housed. "Singapore is now, more than ever, divided into two cities, two populations: the foreign workers in dormitories, and the rest of us".

> This sort of arrangement can be justified ethically only with a geographic bifurcation: The worker is earning money he could never dream of back home. We are not supposed to think of his life here; we are supposed to think about his life there.

She added that the "cheerful certainty" of money flowing into that other life makes all of this "degradation excusable", even beneficial. "But that's a thought exercise. The virus works in flesh and blood, and it has destroyed the fantasy of a disconnected labour pool".

The local and regional response to Stack's commentary, coming as it did when all of us were marooned inside our houses, was immediate and withering. To provide some context, the column appeared during a month when much of America, Stack's home country was in a state of turmoil. I lived through that period in Washington D.C. and can testify to shortages of essential products like masks and bleach and the chaos in the Federal government's early handling of the pandemic. Sitting in Singapore or other Asian capitals, American mismanagement was obvious, which Stack, to be

DOI: 10.4324/9781003603375-7

fair, referenced in her column. However, Singaporeans clearly resented the fact that an American journalist was lecturing them about how to handle the pandemic and passing judgement on their shortcomings. Writing in *Medium,* blogger Ivan Hong[2] passed his own judgement about the Stack column, dissecting every word and provided a strong defence of the government's actions. Here is Hong on Stack's point that "people are filmed constantly" by an army of surveillance cameras.

> I can only imagine how privileged you must feel, Megan, to have the NSA[3] as the vigilant defender of American's privacy, or how proud you must be to consent to your most private activities being scrutinised daily by the most morally-upstanding, all-American charity organisations we know as Apple, Amazon, Google, Twitter, or Facebook.

The sarcasm in Hong's commentary is obvious and so is the anger that an outsider, who also happens to be American, dared to point fingers at Singapore's handling of the pandemic. During an earlier era, when Singapore and Asia were perhaps less prosperous and confident, a negative commentary appearing in a leading American publication would have led to some soul searching. After all, America was the world's richest and most powerful nation and its journalists and journalism were perceived to adhere to the highest professional standards anywhere in the world. Because American power, success, innovation, enterprise, and culture so dominated our collective mind-space (and to a great extent it still does today), journalists or even stand-up comics from the country had a free license to commentate on the many ills and shortcomings of the countries they covered or happened to come by on a brief visit or even from afar. In a world of differing values and standards, America dominated the high moral ground all by itself.

For much of the 20th century and well into the 21st, American exceptionalism held remarkably well and the country's power and influence ensured that it had a word, sometimes even the last word, in determining global economic and political outcomes. That era has definitely passed as we have discovered in the previous chapter and the emerged world is less receptive today to listening to American or European sermons about democracy or economic management.

Idealistic Americans often describe their country as being a "shining city on the hill", offering shelter, refuge, and opportunity for immigrants aspiring to build a better life in the "land of opportunity". Here is the late President Ronald Reagan describing[4] what he means by America being the shining city on a hill.

> But in my mind it was a tall, proud city built on rocks stronger than oceans, wind-swept, God-blessed, and teeming with people of all kinds living in

> harmony and peace: a city with free ports that hummed with commerce and creativity. And if there had to be city walls, the walls had doors and the doors were open to anyone with the will and the heart to get there.

Hopes of fulfilling the American dream, of success and opportunity, has been a powerful magnet for talent from all over the world. America is also home to a large population of illegal migrants, who risk danger and their life savings to make the perilous journey across the Mexican border. American ideals of democracy, rule of law, technocratic competence, strong governance have so permeated the world's consciousness that people begin to notice when these high principles stopped working in that country or are challenged by the superpower's own citizens. And as the response to the Stack commentary in Singapore shows, the rest of the world believes that they too have come of age with increased wealth and confidence and will not be lectured to by American officials and journalists.

This is not a rhetorical point, as I will explain shortly, but represents a fundamental battle of ideas which will determine the course of world affairs in the next few decades. Scholars of a previous era have described this tussle of ideas as representing a genuine clash of civilisations. The late American political scientist Samuel Huntington posited in 1996 that the coming decades will see a world in conflict between "eight civilisations", emphasising that "values, culture, and institutions pervasively influence how states define their interests", adding that "states with similar cultures and institutions will see common interest".

Under Huntington's neat thesis, he listed the world's eight civilisations – the west, Latin America, Orthodox, the eastern world, the Muslim world, sub-Saharan Africa, "lone" countries (Ethiopia, Haiti), and "cleft countries", where large groups of people identifying with separate civilisations (Ukraine, Kenya, Sri Lanka, and others) – implying that the Western grouping would inevitably see itself in conflict with perhaps the Muslim world or Latin America.

For a brief moment after the September 11, 2001, attacks by terror group Al-Qaeda against America, it seemed as though Huntington's thesis would prove to be accurate. That war, also described as a clash of civilisations by headline writers, positioned the west in battle against radical Islamic groups in Afghanistan, Iraq, and many other countries. However, the Islamic groups were not acting in concert with countries with vast Muslim majorities, whose citizens themselves were subjected to attacks by the same groups, diluting a significant part of the thesis. As Chinese scholar Tian Dewen[5] notes, the use of cultural differences to explain international conflicts may not be unreasonable, but it is also not new.

> The "clash of civilisations" is characterised by pushing the effects of cultural differences to the extreme, emphasising that not only differences

> between civilisations will become the deep causes of international conflicts, but also that groups of states will form within civilisational blocs to confront other civilisations,

he writes, "This is a cut-and-dried argument based on the logical fallacy of taking "correlation" as "casualty", and as a result the "clash of civilisations" cannot explain the true causes of international conflicts in the post-Cold War era".

Where Huntington's thesis has also not stood the test of time is within his favoured grouping itself, the west. He failed to see that in America and Europe, a very different clash of civilisations and cultures would unfold, pitting *internal groups* and factions at ideological war with each other. In America, this has resulted in the remarkable and improbable rise of Donald Trump as the defender of his country's nationalist, nativist, and populist interests which are at war with what his supporters deride as globalist elites. Here is Steve Bannon, one of Trump's ideologues, describing the failings of the globalist elite in response to a question from *The New York Times*[6]:

> Well, I think it's very simple: that the ruling elites of the west lost confidence in themselves. The elites have lost faith in their countries. They've lost faith in the Westphalian[7] system, the nation-state. They are more and more detached from the lived experience of their people.

Bannon's thesis, which has resonated and gained wide currency in America thanks to Donald Trump, is that a globalist elite ecosystem comprising corporate leaders, journalists, unelected bureaucrats, politicians, technologists, and financiers essentially hijacked the American dream in favour of unbridled globalisation – where factories were shut in America to migrate to China because of lower wages and lesser red tape, creating massive social displacement at home. Ideologues like Bannon believe that America's support for China's accession to the WTO in 2001 was a massive foreign and public policy failure because it essentially hollowed out America's trade and manufacturing base and facilitated the rise of China as a manufacturing powerhouse and a serious rival to America. Here is Bannon again, in a separate interview,[8] describing Trump's populist appeal.

> It's both cultural and economic, but it's really a push against an established order that's truly globalist in nature and has really lost touch with the American people, with the working class and lower middle class in this country. They are the backbone of this country.

The first and second Trump administration's war against the established American order, also known as the "deep state", has supplanted traditional beliefs about how a superpower should wield power and influence at home and abroad. It is America first and last, an idea which has gained wide resonance within the electorate and has the potential to fundamentally transform the incumbent superpower's relations with the world. Trump's America is both mercantilist, in terms of advancing the country's economic interests at the expense of everyone else, and transactional, in terms of cutting a tactical deal in exchange for access to the country's vast internal market. The currency that the President deploys is tariffs, plenty of it, to ensure submission by the country's trading partners.

> My message to every business in the world is very simple. Come make your product in America, and we will give you among the lowest taxes of any nation on Earth. We're bringing them down very substantially even from the original Trump tax cuts,

the newly inaugurated Trump told the World Economic Forum at Davos in January 2025

> But it you don't make your product in America, which is your prerogative, then, very simply, you will have to pay a tariff – differing amounts, but a tariff – which will direct hundreds of billions of dollars and even trillions of dollars into our Treasury to strengthen our economy and pay down debt.

The Trump thesis is a sharp rebuttal and reversal of the greatest American idea of them all – that globalisation, free trade, and investment were uniformly positive and a universal public good, which America in its benevolence, had gifted to the world by providing unlimited market access. Never mind the fact that America produced or exported little in volume to match the gush of imports of products and services into the country. This resulted in the country generating huge trade deficits year-on-year (an estimated $300 billion with China alone in 2023) and a huge budget deficit (an estimated $1.83 trillion in 2024 or a whopping 6.4% of GDP). Thanks to the dollar's primacy as the world's unchallenged reserve currency, the US has managed to plug that deficit by borrowing huge amounts from willing foreign creditors, an estimated $36 trillion or 123% of GDP from reserve surplus countries like China and others in East Asia who park their money in US Treasuries. The Trump agenda is aimed at sweeping the slate clean – by sharply increasing trade tariffs and over time reducing the trade deficit and overall debt. From a national self-interest point of view this is an understandable objective, although Trump's incendiary and chaotic, transactional management style often run counter to his economic objectives.

The question for emerged countries is this – if the most reliable and stable provider of global public goods, America, turns its back to the globalised world it essentially created, do these countries have the capability and capacity to build an alternative world order where globalisation, trade, and investment continue to flourish? The answer from China is an affirmative yes while other large countries like India, Brazil, and South Africa would prefer to have it both ways i.e. retaining continued access to the American market while developing alternative sources of growth. Focusing on Asia, the World Economic Forum notes[9] that the region is experiencing an era of increased intraregional connectivity and cooperation.

> Global businesses, as well as East Asian multinationals (including those based in China) are moving manufacturing and sourcing to Southeast Asia. These nations are well connected – both with each other and to major markets around the world – which has created opportunities for companies to build integrated supply chains and tap markets across the region.

The Forum report emphasised that new regional trade agreements in the region are reinforcing this change. Both the Regional Comprehensive Economic Partnership (RCEP), which includes China, New Zealand, Australia, Korea, Asean, and Japan, and the Comprehensive and Progressive Agreement for Trans-Pacific Partnership (CPTPP), which includes many of the RCEP countries excluding China, are aimed at building a reliable and robust trade partnership between member countries. America of course is the notable absentee in these groupings, having withdrawn from CPTPP's predecessor Trans-Pacific Partnership (TPP) in the aftermath of Trump's first election victory in 2016. America's absence is the vital missing link in expanding global commerce, and it is questionable if Asia or Europe on their own can serve as reliable guardians of globalisation. America has upended the rules and terms (unless it is reversed by a future administration), and the world will have to live with the consequences.

However, there are other aspects of Americana – democracy, the rule of law, inclusive capitalism, which we will deal with in turn – which may provide to be even more resilient in other corners of the world in contrast with their relative decline in America. Like hamburgers and French fries, America has long been associated with democracy at home and its relentless advocacy overseas. From John F. Kennedy to Joseph Biden, American Presidents have been tireless champions and salesmen for democratic ideals. During Biden's tenure, he even convened a Summit for Democracy in December 2021[10] and acknowledged that American democracy is an "ongoing struggle" to live up to the country's highest ideals. "Democracy doesn't happen by accident", the President said, "We have to renew it with each generation. And this is an urgent matter on all of our parts, in my view.

Because the data we're seeing is largely pointing in the wrong direction". There was a tinge of irony in the former President's speech because the single, greatest threat to democracy today originates in America itself, with robust nationalist voices led by President Trump questioning the wisdom of cherished democratic traditions like accountability, checks and balances, and elections itself. President Trump himself famously refused to accept his electoral defeat to Biden in the 2020, and while he has furiously denied any involvement, the deadly riots in the Capitol in Washington D.C. on January 6, 2021, happened under his watch.

Dictators all over the world will draw comfort from the Trump thesis that elections are fair when he wins (as he did in 2016 and 2024) and rigged and fraudulent (when he lost in 2020). America's electoral system and the judiciary have proven itself to be durable, for now, against these accusations but the question remains for how long? In striking contrast, there are large, democratic nations in Asia which are holding the candle for free and fair elections and where the electorate is enthusiastic and buys into the proposition that there will be winners and losers. I was born and raised in one (India) and worked in the other (Indonesia) and they are a test to the durability of democracy in the next few decades. There are of course serious problems in both countries about how democratic principles are actually put to practice. Under Prime Minister Modi, the ruling BJP has weaponised the judiciary to go after political rivals and to silence the media. Although Indonesia's embrace of democracy in 1998, a momentous event which I witnessed first-hand as a journalist, has proven to be resilient, the ruling class appears determined to establish a system where there is no genuine opposition and all political parties share in the spoils. The only option for disgruntled voters in both countries is either to take to the streets in protest (as has happened in Delhi and Jakarta with increasing frequency) or to exercise their franchise in the voting booth.

The statistics for India's recent elections are staggering. Here are some eye-popping numbers from *Reuters*[11] on the 2024 electoral process. About 642 million eligible Indian voters cast their ballots in the seven-phase polling over six weeks, the largest election in history. "The world's biggest election involved over one million polling stations spread across the country, from remote corners of the Himalayas to far-flung forests deep in Nagaland. Each polling station served a maximum of 1500 people". The process involved over 15 million people, 400,000 vehicles, nearly 1,700 air sorties, and 135 trains moving across the country. Most importantly, electronic voting machines (EVMs) have been deployed in Indian elections since 1982 and are not a source of suspicion or contention, as it has become in America. I agree that the holding of elections alone does not necessarily guarantee a robust democratic system. However, the fact that over 600 million Indian voters showed up in the summer of 2024 and deprived the ruling BJP of a majority sent a powerful signal that elections have consequences.

The election process in neighbouring Indonesia is equally impressive. While Indonesians are relative newcomers to democracy, having only secured rights after the ouster of President Suharto in 1998, they are equally enthusiastic about the overall process. Indonesia holds the record for conducting the world's largest single-day elections, with over 200 million voters exercising their franchise across the vast archipelagic country. Voter turnout in the most recent polls was an impressive 82%, compared with India's 66% and America's 63% in the same year.

Now democracy enthusiasts in America will read this section and push-back against the proposition that the electoral systems in India and Indonesia are perhaps more robust compared with the world's superpower. It is absolutely true that the electoral process in the two democracies is dogged by allegations of voter intimidation, suppression, and what in India is charmingly described as "booth capturing".[12]

The sad fact is that such practices are proliferating in America too. Don't take my word for it. Here is Freedom House,[13] the august American democracy watch-dog, describing the proliferation of three blatantly anti-democratic, voter suppression tactics which have become the norm. First is the upsurge in harassment and intimidation of election workers since the 2020 election, which is all too familiar in the emerged world. Second is "partisan meddling" in the process of certifying election results, which used to be a routine exercise until it was weaponised by partisan politicians. Finally, "misleading election-fraud narratives" have been used as "pretexts" for changes to election policies in certain states, which restrict voter access.

> But if the new restrictions are based on false claims about election-security risks, the question remains why create any potential new barriers to voters' access to the polls, even minor ones, when there is so little evidence of fraud in the first place.

Freedom House's Mark Iglesias argues.

In many parts of the emerged world, Freedom House is associated with its annual rankings on democracy, which rankles many countries because it is seen as judging the world from a particularly American perspective. It is refreshing to see that the watch-dog is focusing attention on electoral suppression and abuses at home as well. In India and Indonesia's defence, it must be said that no opposition leader or politician has seriously questioned the legitimacy of the electoral process as Trump has done with spectacular effect in America. If American leadership is faltering, what about Europe that second powerful beacon of democracy and freedoms?

The sad reality is that while Europeans continue to preach about their continent's unique democratic proposition, the wheels are literally falling off at home. From the UK to France to Germany, far-right political parties are gaining political power, with countries like Italy and Hungary already under the thrall of parties which preach cultural exceptionalism and are fiercely against immigration. Yet the European proclivity to preach overseas remains undiminished. In a cheeky column in February 2025, *The Economist*[14] suggested that India could serve as a model for the European Union (EU). "For all of India's flaws, an attentive European visitor will see much that should make them envious – and that they might learn from. Once under the thumb of European colonisers, India is an unexpected role model for today's EU". This is because of India's high rates of economic growth compared with the sickly pace in Europe, the country's youthful demographics, and a model for the EU, which is struggling to build cohesion amongst 27 disparate member states, in terms of building unity through diversity, India's remarkable achievement.

But old preaching habits die hard. A few years ago, Indian opposition Parliamentarian Shashi Tharoor recounted a visit to Brussels where he was pressed to advocate for an EU-India free trade agreement, which has been talked about and negotiated for over a decade with little progress. One of the major reasons for the deadlock, according to Tharoor, was the EU's insistence that there should be a human rights chapter in the FTA, ostensibly embedding commitments from the Indian side to adhere to certain human rights obligations. Now, the Modi government should be held accountable for the many human rights violations that have taken place under its watch. However, attempting to include human rights issues in a free trade agreement will only embolden the government to declare that the allegations are either false or exaggerated. In the 2024 elections, Indian voters in their wisdom decided that the ruling BJP had not delivered on their promises and decided to take away their majority in Parliament. As Americans and Europeans will appreciate, there is no greater democratic principle when citizens chose to elect or eject political parties into and from office. The hectoring and preaching from the west has the unintended result of political leaders rallying their populations against foreign interference. There are exceptional cases of course where external pressure and intervention is not only desirable but essential. This includes cases where opposition leaders or dissidents are detained for long periods without cause or trial, as happened with Myanmar leader Aung San Suu Kyi in the 1990s.

I must add that Western countries are often well-meaning in their advocacy of democracy and the rule of law. But many leaders simply don't recognise that countries they perceived to be underdeveloped even a decade ago have come of age and will not be pushed around. As illustrated in the case of democracy, the west is also in the breach when it comes to rules and norms governing capitalism. I have recounted this story in my previous books but worth repeating here as well. In 1997 and 1998, I was a journalist based in Jakarta, Indonesia, around the time that country, along with many others in the region, faced a severe economic shock. The Asian financial crisis of that era today merits only a footnote in the global economic discourse. For countries in the region it was a profoundly shocking moment when they realised that the raw capitalism which they had pursed had disastrous economic, social, and political consequences.

What went wrong? In a word, it had a lot to do with unbridled, unchecked capitalism, where governments in pursuit of high economic growth overlooked the negative aspects of letting domestic banks and the corporate sector access foreign capital with very little restraints. There are many complicated reasons why Indonesia and other Asian crisis casualties – Thailand, the Philippines, and Korea – fell spectacularly during the summer of 1997. Erosion of foreign investor confidence was one of the popular reasons cited at the time, particularly in the brand of "crony capitalism" practised by businesses in the crisis countries.

Crony capitalism was short-hand for American and European commentators to criticise the lack of strong corporate governance standards in East Asia, including poor transparency and disclosure rules, and collusion between favoured business groups and the state.

> The essential argument of the Greenspan-Summers-IMF[15] thesis (GSI thesis) was that poor corporate governance mechanisms and poor competition as well as crony capitalism enabled Asian firms to disregard profits in their pursuit of market share, leading to over-investment, which in turn generated a crisis,

an interesting research paper from Cambridge University argued in 2006. Cambridge researchers[16] added that it was on the basis of this analysis, that IMF economists recommended changes in "fundamental institutions" of the Asian crisis nations. Their prescription, hold your breath, was astonishing.

> Essentially, developing countries were advised to abandon the Asian business model and adopt in its place the US model based on shareholders' wealth maximisation subject to the discipline of liquid stock markets. Thus, they were expected to change their institutions of corporate governance, their labour laws, financial system based on "relationship lending", and, more generally, the nature of the relationship between government, business, and finance. In the IMF view, its advocacy of a US-type model was based on the ostensible superior ability of such a model to allocate resources and monitor corporate behaviour.

The timing of the Cambridge paper, June 2006, was prescient because very few policymakers and commentators expressed scepticism or warned about the durability of the American economic and financial model at the time. The prevailing idea was that American capitalism was inherently superior to other economic models, and vulnerabilities building up on the overall system were ignored or derided as alarmists. One of the sceptics was Raghuram Rajan, who even earlier in 2005, published a paper[17] warning that unchecked financialisation of the US economy had made the world riskier. Rajan was the IMF's Chief Economist at the time, and I had a first-hand view of how more powerful economists and policymakers in Washington D.C. underplayed or criticised Rajan for his perceived alarmist approach. We all know how this story ended in spectacular fashion in September 2008, when the US Treasury's decision not to save Lehman Brothers triggered the global financial crisis (GFC). The origins of the GFC were in the US housing sector, and just like the crisis in Asia a decade earlier, it exposed shortcomings and weaknesses in corporate governance and financial sector supervision, of course on a much grander scale because of the global impact. Strangely enough, as highlighted before, the financial systems of emerged countries were largely intact during the GFC, suggesting that they perhaps learnt lessons from the Asian crisis while the rest of the world did not.

The rise of crony capitalism in America, which has now become mainstream, is even more tragic. During President Trump's second inauguration in January 2025, the second most powerful group in the US Capitol were not Republican politicians. It was a tech billionaire group headed by Elon Musk and included Meta's Mark Zuckerberg, Amazon's Jeff Bezos, and others who received prominent seating close to the President.[18] The fact that Musk himself contributed over $250 million to the Trump election campaign and the other billionaires made $1 million donations for the privilege of attending the inauguration suggests that American capitalism has returned to its late 19th-century roots, where the phrase robber baron originated.[19] Nobel Prize winning economist Paul Krugman writes[20] that political spending by the "tech bros" could have huge effects on US politics. "In short, the tech bro style in American politics has emerged as a major force, one that, in my view, is pushing our democracy closer to catastrophe".

As *The Economist* has suggested, it is time for Europe (and the US) to cast aside their perceptions and prejudices about the emerged world and even perhaps learn from them. This is not a zero-sum game. There are many, many areas where the rich Western nations still excel. However, the game-changer for the global economy, at least since the GFC, has been the dominance of emerged countries in certain industrial and digital sectors. We will turn to these case studies in the next three chapters. America and Europe, start taking notes.

Notes

1 *The New York Times* column by Megan K. Stack, May 20, 2020.
2 How *The New York Times*' put a racist spin on Singapore's COVID-19 efforts, Ivan Hong, Medium, May 21, 2020.
3 For the uninitiated, NSA is America's National Security Agency which is tasked with communications-related surveillance.
4 Ronald Reagan, Farewell Address, January 11, 1989. Source: Ronald Reagan Presidential Library and Museum.
5 What's wrong with the "clash of civilisations" – Tian Dewen, China Watch, Volume 2, No. 5, February 2022.
6 My unsettling interview with Steve Bannon – David Brooks, *The New York Times*, July 1, 2024.
7 This refers to the original principle developed after the 1648 Peace of Westphalia, which essentially states that nation-states have the powers over internal matters and no outside force has the right to intervene.
8 Steve Bannon on "Broligarchs" vs. Populism –*The New York Times*, January 31, 2025.
9 Why Asia's time is now" what's fuelling Asian growth and what does it mean for the rest of the world? – World Economic Forum, June 24, 2024.
10 Remarks by President Biden at the Summit for Democracy opening session – December 9, 2021.
11 How India conducted the world's largest election – Reuters, June 6, 2024.
12 Booth capturing in Indian elections essentially means the takeover of an electoral polling station by a group of thugs at the behest of a political party and with the intent of stealing votes.
13 As False Election Narratives Multiply, Several Promising Initiatives are Working to Defend the Democratic Process – Freedom House, September 19, 2024.
14 How India became an unexpected role model for Europe –*The Economist*, February 13, 2025.
15 Greenspan refers to Alan Greenspan, the long serving former Chair of the Federal Reserve, Summers is Larry Summers, who served as deputy Treasury Secretary during the Asian crisis.
16 Corporate governance, crony capitalism, and economic crisis – Should the US business model replace the Asian way of doing business – Working Paper No. 329 by Ajit Singh and Ann Zammit, Centre for Business Research, University of Cambridge, June 2006.
17 Has financial development made the world riskier – by Raghuram Rajan, National Bureau of Economic Research Working Paper, November 2005.
18 Also present at the inauguration was Indian billionaire Mukesh Ambani.
19 The August 1870 issue of The Atlantic Monthly magazine first used the phrase robber baron to describe a group of businessmen of that era who had accumulated power and influence, often through unscrupulous means.
20 The Tech Bro style in American Politics – Paul Krugman, The New York Times, September 26, 2024.

Section II

The Case Studies

Chapter 6

China

EVs

How did China come to dominate the global market for electric vehicles and the entire supply chain?

When I was a business journalist in India in the 1980s, we were awe-struck by the long-form journalism originating from America, which examined in depth every aspect of American and global business. One of the defining screeds of that era, at least for business journalists of a certain age, was David Halberstam's towering work of narrative non-fiction on the eclipse of the American automobile industry and the rise of Japan's nimble car producers led by Nissan.

Even today, decades after it was published, *The Reckoning*[1] remains a relevant work of non-fiction because it documents the precise moment in the late 1960s when American car-makers became complacent about their dominance of the home market. Halberstam documents their arrogance in painstaking detail. The opening paragraph sets it up very well. "There had been plenty of warnings", he writes

> Some experts had pointed out that the sources of oil were not limitless, that consumption was rising faster than production. Some noted that certain of the oil-producing countries were politically unstable and hostile to the United States. The men of the auto industry had never heeded the warnings. They dismissed them as veiled criticisms of the cars they were making.

During that heady decade, America's Big Three car-makers (Ford, General Motors, Chrysler) produced over 8 million cars annually, outpacing the production of European rivals. These cars also happened to be designed for an era of Easy Oil, they were gas-guzzlers which consumed huge quantities of petrol. In 1973, just before the Arab oil embargo crushed Detroit

DOI: 10.4324/9781003603375-9

with a dramatic increase in oil prices, the car-makers ignored warnings that their business model was about to be challenged.

When the Arab oil embargo hit, it was a group of car manufacturers across the Pacific who capitalised on the major shift in consumer attitudes and preferences in America. Out went the gas-guzzlers made by Ford and GM and in came the agile Datsun and a stable of cheap, fuel-efficient Japanese imports which soon flooded the country. While American car-makers were asleep at the wheel and failed to anticipate a major shift in geopolitics and energy demand, Halberstam writes that the Japanese government and car-makers were extremely well prepared for this moment. He profiles a senior bureaucrat of Japan's elite Ministry of Trade and Industry (MITI) who in the late 1960s began to fret about the price of oil. MITI was then at the peak of its powers and influence in shaping corporate outcomes,

> The Japanese economy, Amaya recognised in the late sixties, was perched on something terribly volatile, the world price of oil. What was worse, its oil came from sources that were totally alien to Japan. Only Arab sheiks, Texas oilmen, and acts of God could determine the price of oil, Amaya liked to say, and they were all beyond Japan's control.

When asked by the government to study the energy situation and examine its potential impact, Amaya arrived at a contrarian, counter-intuitive conclusion at that time.

> More and more countries, he decided, were coming into what he had called the "oil culture"; that is, they were making their economies, indeed their way of life, dependent upon oil. He believed that sooner or later the price would explode, perhaps doubling or even quadrupling, and if that happened, it would devastate the Japanese economy.

Amaya's foresight did not prevent the oil embargo from devastating the Japanese economy, as all oil-importing countries of that era faced the full wrath of the action by Saudi Arabia and other oil-rich nations. However, it essentially created the conditions for the rise of Japanese car-makers as a global force because they were the only ones at the time who were producing reasonably priced, fuel-efficient cars which precisely matched consumer demand. After being laughed at for producing ugly, small cars during much of the 1960s, Japanese car-makers had the last laugh during the following decade with Toyota, Nissan, Honda, Subaru, and others capturing market share from inefficient American rivals. Chrysler almost went bust, and mighty Ford and GM were forced to painfully adapt to the changing needs of the market-place.

If all of this sounds familiar with the current moment, the sobering fact is that history appears to repeat itself in the global automobile industry, neither as a tragedy or farce but as a dramatic manifestation of an Asian country's rise as an automobile super-power. From 1973, let's turn the clock forwards to 2016. It was the year China was hosting the G20, the gathering of leaders of the world's largest economies. The setting was Hangzhou, the beautiful lake-side city and home to some of the country's impressive private sector stars like Alibaba. I was working for an international bank at the time and attending the Business 20 summit which took place on the sidelines of the political gathering. It seemed like Jack Ma was everywhere at the summit, expounding on the virtues of Chinese entrepreneurship and the technological edge which his country was gaining over American rivals.

While Ma and Alibaba were all show, bank executives decided to visit a quiet corner of Hangzhou to meet with senior executives of Geely, a fast-rising automobile manufacturer. It must be said that the notion that China, recently risen from poverty, was able to produce world-beating cars was regarded with amusement those days. But the car-maker's founder clearly had a plan and a vision for his fledgeling car company, which had started out making refrigerator parts. In 2016, Geely was virtually unknown outside of China. The company had acquired a stake in Volvo and was rapidly building minority ownership in other leading car manufacturers – Mercedes Benz, Aston Martin – and was still producing conventional, fossil fuel cars.

The presentation laid out by the senior leadership of the company has stayed with me. In a quiet, methodical style, a corporate executive said that Geely had three aspirations. First, to dominate China's automobile industry. Second, to dominate the global automobile industry in terms of quality. Third, to do both by producing electric vehicles (EVs) and by contributing to the decarbonisation of the global economy. I came away from that meeting with mixed views. I surmised that Geely would either emerge as the second-famous global company from Hangzhou or the painstaking detail offered in the presentation was all hype. My first instinct that Geely executives were not kidding about their global ambitions proved to be the more accurate prediction. The numbers are staggering.

In 2024, Geely sold 3.36 million vehicles globally, 1.48 million of them in EVs, a rise of 52% over the previous year. Overseas sales also touched 1.22 million. Although not the world's largest car manufacturer, Geely has come a long way. This pattern is repeated in the performance of Geely's domestic rivals, some of whom like BYD are significantly larger than the Hangzhou producer. BYD founder Wang Chuangfu is another larger-than-life auto titan who has emerged from China in recent years. The company is expected to sell 5 million cars in 2025, including over

1 million overseas. Wang is "more of disrupter than many had expected", says Ilara Mazzocco,[2] of the DC-based Center for Strategic and International Studies, "He's an empire builder; people should think about him in the same category as Bezos or Musk".

How times have changed. Writing in *The New York Times,*[3] economist Brad Setser notes that around 20 years ago, China was a "nonfactor" in automaking. "By 2018, it had the capacity to produce 40 million gasoline-powered cars per year, far more than the 25 million its economy needed", Setser writes

> Since then, it has added thanks in part to substantial government subsidies for the industry, the capacity to make 20 million electric vehicles annually, a number that may soon rise to 30 million. Annual global automotive demand is 90 million cars: China has the capacity to produce around two-thirds of that.

The last line may be an over-statement because the sheer ability to produce cars at scale, which China has clearly demonstrated, does not necessarily translate into global success in the marketplace. That would require a sustained, long-term investment in the consumer side of the business including building a global brand reputed for quality and reliability.

As things stand, Chinese car-makers appear to be learning the right lessons and learning them fast. In Dubai, cars on the road which usually draw out-sized attention are the Bentley's, the Rolls Royce's, and the Ferraris. In recent years, China-made cars have been getting considerable attention and purchase from the consumer, not because they are Uber luxury sedans, but the simple fact is that they are more competitively priced compared with conventional brands like Toyota and Hyundai. From being virtually unknown before the pandemic, Chinese car brands like Zeekr (made by Geely), BYD, Neo, and Jetour have become ubiquitous on Dubai's clogged streets. This phenomenon has been replicated in many parts of the emerged world where China-made cars are more welcome compared with the tariff barriers placed on them in America and Europe. I even spotted a swanky BYD showroom in Mumbai, India, although that country briefly froze economic ties in the aftermath of the 2020 border attacks with China.

While China produces both conventional fossil fuel and electric vehicles, it has clearly established a dominant lead in the latter, both in the full battery electric vehicle (BEV) and plug-in hybrid (PHEV) segments. Market intelligence firm *Adamas Inside*[4] estimates that in 2023, China was responsible for 58% of the 13.7 million BEVs and PHEVs sold globally.

> That's five times the size of the US market and seven times that of the world's third largest EV market, Germany. Despite the size of China's EV

> market, EV penetration rates in the country reached 22% last year, versus 15% in the US, excluding conventional hybrid electric vehicles (HEVs).

This implies that China still has a considerable way to go in achieving deep penetration rates in its own market and also has the ability to flex its production muscle by taking market share from global auto majors in developed and developing markets. How did this come to be? What were the factors which led to the rise of China's automotive industry, which many observers dismissed as uncompetitive a few years ago?

It is useful to explore this by using the same reporting and research tools deployed by the late David Halberstam over four decades ago. China's EV success as we will unpack shortly is due to a combination of factors – industrial policy, manufacturing prowess, supply chain dominance, generous state subsidies, and a savagely competitive domestic market reeling from over-capacity and beggar-your-competitor pricing policies.

Let's start at the beginning though in 2000, when even the notion of producing fully electric vehicles at scale was regarded as pie-in-the-sky thinking by the world's car majors. Just three years earlier, in 1997, Japan's Toyota had launched the Prius, the world's first gasoline-electric hybrid car in its home market and rolled it out globally in 2000. Toyota explains that its primary objective in rolling out the Prius was to improve fuel efficiency, to a level 1.5 times that of conventional engines. Environmental considerations may have been a factor but not explicitly set out in the company's own historical record[5] of the genesis of Prius. This explains the shift in emphasis from what would have been a full electric model into a hybrid variant.

> In addition to improving the efficiency of the engine and driving system, epoch making functions such as energy regeneration and stopping the engine while the vehicle is stationery were also employed in order to realise a high fuel efficiency of 30km/L, approximately double that of other vehicles in the same class (at the time 1995).

When Prius hit global markets in 2000, it was regarded as a revolutionary concept, indeed it was promoted as the "car for the 21st century". Consumers rewarded Toyota's innovation with record purchases of the car in the first decade of the new century and the car continues to do well, despite rising competition. The Japanese company estimates that since the brand was launched in 1997, over 6 million of them have been sold worldwide, making it one of the most successful vehicle brands ever. Yet, as the company continued to produce various models of the hybrid, it was painfully slow to adapt to the fully electric vehicle segment, where China now dominates. Indeed, of the estimated 9 million cars which it produces annually, fully electric vehicles account for a tiny portion of sales. The company's communications on its EV strategy have been ambiguous at best. As an article in *Time* explains,[6] the notion that Toyota was going to leapfrog the EV industry was "dead".

> That sort of ambiguity – perhaps of a strategic sort – has been the general tone of Toyota's climate communication over the past year. Before that, for the past couple years, the company has been regarded as among the worst laggards in the auto industry's green transition. It was an odd designation for an auto player that brought the world the first mass-market hybrid electric car, the Prius, in 1997.

The parallels are striking – between Halberstam's documentation of the rise of Japan's automobile industry in the 1960s (while American car producers slept) and Japan's own sleepwalking several decades later, while China perfected the production of EVs. The historic context behind China's rise is interesting.

As it strengthened its manufacturing prowess as factory of the world, Chinese policymakers in the late 1990s realised that it would take a leap of faith and significant state resources to establish a world-beating automobile industry. According to an analysis by the *MIT Technology Review,*[7] in the early 2000s, the country realised that despite having a developed auto industry, it faced a "near impossible task" in seeking to challenge the pre-eminence in making traditional internal combustion engine vehicles enjoyed by manufacturers from the US, Germany, and Japan – "the latter which had established a lead in hybrid vehicles".

During my first visit to China, circa 1994, my reference point at the time was both Singapore (where I was working) and India (where I am from). While Singapore's roads were the epitome of cutting-edge automobile technology, I was equally familiar with India's leap from car obscurity, where the only cars available were outdated versions of the Morris Oxford Series (produced in the UK in the 1950s) and the Fiat. By the time, I visited Shanghai for the first time, India was undergoing an automobile revolution with the presence of Japanese and European car majors. It seemed like the auto industry in India would progress faster than China, which since the 1980s only produced the boxy Volkswagen Santana, which were less ubiquitous on Shanghai streets compared with the humble bicycle, the transportation of choice for millions of the city's residents. If you had asked me in 1994 if "car culture" would ever take off in China, compared with America, I would have been sceptical. China had just emerged from the horrors of Tiananmen Square, and car ownership by individuals was still unaffordable and even frowned upon. Yet six years later, Chinese authorities proved the sceptics like me wrong and embarked on an ambitious push to invest in the automobile industry, with the full intention of making cars accessible to the country's 1.4 billion citizens and perhaps even take on the world. In the process, China left India's car manufacturers and indeed much of the world far behind.

The Abdul Latif Jameel (ALJ) group, which also supports a poverty action laboratory at Harvard University, has published a fascinating historic analysis of China's rise as a major global car manufacturer. It argues[8] that in 2000, China took the "alternative and high-risk" approach on focusing on pure EVs as the platform to build its auto industry.

> In 2001, the government made EV technology a priority science research project in its five-year plan, which sets out the country's high-level economic strategy. In 2007, Wan Gang, previously an engineer at Audi in Germany and a champion of EVs, was appointed minister of science and technology. Wan's influence is seen by many as crucial in China's consistent prioritization of EVs.

The notion that an influential technocrat like Wan was shaping and influencing industrial policy and private sector investment was an alien concept in the west until recently. Industrial policy and state planning were regarded as a statist, and Amaya *san,* Japan's MITI technocrat who features in Halberstam's book, was equally derided for meddling in capitalism and private enterprise. We have come full circle on this thinking of course with both America and Europe launching massive industrial policy efforts in recent years, including state subsidies, some of it to counter China's growing dominance in areas like EVs, solar, and advanced technology.

There is no doubt that China has massively subsidised the production of EVs. The ALJ assessment notes that the Chinese government sees the EV industry as strategically important and has supported its development through a range of "well-funded policy measures" to boost both supply and demand.

> Between 2009 and 2022, it spent more than 200 billion yuan (around \$28 billion) on EV subsidies and tax breaks. Until 2022, for example, buyers of EVs could benefit from a reimbursement of up to 60,000 yuan (around \$8000). Many local governments continue to generously subsidise EV purchases,

according to ALJ. To top this, in 2023, the national government unveiled a four-year package extending tax breaks for EV buyers, worth 520 billion yuan (more than \$72 billion). EVs and other green cars will continue to be exempt from purchase tax in 2024 and 2025, with the rate halved for following years. I have verified the data for China's EV subsidies from other sources, and they all add up to the ALJ number. I must add that the Chinese government has also provided direct subsidies for EV manufacturers, which has enabled BYD, which received around 2 billion yuan, or $275 million, to edge out Tesla as the world's largest EV producer.

There are two ways of reacting to this data. First, as many Western commentators like Setser have done, to react with shock and fury that China was subsidising the EV industry and encouraging its manufacturers to dump vehicles at extremely competitive prices in global markets. Chinese EVs are no doubt price competitive in most markets I am familiar with. While BYD's Atto 3 is not available in the US, its indicative retail price, according to industry bible *Carsguide,* would be around $34,540. Its direct competitor in the US is Tesla's Model 3, which averages around $45,000. The comparison is imperfect because the car industry is notoriously non-transparent when it comes to pricing. In the UAE, the Atto 3 retails at around 110,000 AED (around $29,000) compared with the Tesla Model 3's 167,000 AED (around $45,000).[9] There is a steep price differential and I can understand the motivations behind the Biden administration's decision to impose import duties of 100% on Chinese-made cars. Europe, already stinging under Chinese car competition, is pursuing a similar path although it is complicated by the fact that many Chinese car producers like BYD are building a manufacturing base in countries like Hungary. China's deep incursions into the European and global market poses an existential threat to European powerhouse Germany, as made-in-China products (automobiles, chemicals, capital goods) flood the market.

Second, while accepting the point that subsidies are uncompetitive and harmful, I would like to offer an alternative way of looking at the issue. Economic history is replete with examples of failed industrial policy initiatives all over the world and subsidies which ended up by becoming a burden on the tax-payer. In Asia itself, Indonesia's ill-fated efforts to build a commercial airplane industry in the 1980s and 1990s were shuttered after the Asian financial crisis, by which time the state had already been pumped in $2 billion in subsidies with little to show by way of progress. India's own light combat aircraft (LCA) project, now relabelled Tejas, struggled mightily since the 1980s to achieve commercial production, by which time the government poured an estimated $110 billion into the development of the fighter aircraft. Tejas is now part of the Indian Air Force's fleet although defence analysts tell me that is hopelessly behind the times. India achieved greater success with the Maruti car project, which was initially a state-owned enterprise but the sale of a stake to Japan's Suzuki corporation enabled the company to emerge as India's largest car manufacturer.

So China deserves some credit for originating the ambition of building EVs to scale and subsidising the production and sale. While the Geely and BYD brands get all of the attention, the secret sauce for China's success has also been in its manufacturing prowess and dominance of the battery supply chain. As highlighted above, China's EV ambitions may well have gone pear shaped if it did not possess the manufacturing platform and capabilities to produce cars at scale. The country was known as "factory to the world" for a good reason. Ask Tim Cook, the CEO of Apple which has used contract manufacturers like Foxconn to mass produce the Apple iPhone and other products for several years. In an old video interview which went viral last year,[10] Cook dismissed the notion that foreign companies flock to China for cheap labour. "There is confusion about China. And let me at least give you my opinion", he said, "The popular conception is that companies come to China because of low labour costs. I am not sure what part of China they go to, but the truth is China stopped being a low labour cost country many years ago". He added that China's technical expertise in several areas was the real reason why Apple was manufacturing in the country.

> The reason is because of the skill, the quantity of skill in one location, and the type of skill it is. And the tooling skill is very deep here. You know, in the US, you could have a meeting of tooling engineers, and I am not sure we could fill the room. In China, you could fill multiple football fields. It's that vocational expertise is very, very deep here.

While Cook has every reason to wax eloquent about the virtues of China's technical expertise, there are persistent allegations about intellectual property theft, not just in smartphone production but in a whole slew of advanced manufacturing like semiconductors and automobiles. The modus operandi apparently, since none of this can be verified independently, is through hacking conducted by shadowy actors linked with China. In April 2024, for example, German auto major Volkswagen suffered a major cybersecurity breach with fingers pointing in the direction of Beijing. "The stolen data encompasses critical information on Volkswagen's proprietary EV technologies, posing a direct threat to its competitive edge in the EV market", says a report from *Secure Blink*,[11] "The hackers' targeted agenda is evident from the theft's specifics, including data on gasoline engine and transmission development, particularly dual-clutch transmissions". The Chinese government has denied this specific allegation, along with many others. I was also amused that within China itself, Geely was awarded significant damages by China's Intellectual Property Court in a case against rival WM Motor as the latter was found involved in "large-scale poaching" of Geely's talent, resulting in the "infringement of trade secrets".[12]

It is the combination of state subsidies and allegations of IP theft which has dampened Western enthusiasm towards China-made products, including cars. However, hiding behind the success is another factor which is receiving huge attention from American and European car-makers aspiring to match China on EVs. This stems from Beijing's absolute dominance of the critical minerals supply chain and in the production of batteries, which are *the* building blocks for the mass production of EVs. We have never heard of companies like Nanjing Hanrui, Zhejiang Huayou, or the CMOC Group, large players in mining cobalt. Fewer people also have vague knowledge about the Democratic Republic of Congo (DRC), the giant but conflicted central African nation which happens to have much of the world's known deposits of copper and cobalt, critical minerals without which electric vehicles would not be a viable business. When America and Europe slept through the 2000s and 2010s, China started accumulating investment interest in faraway DRC (and Indonesia) for the development of nickel and cobalt mines and to feed them to the country's aspirations of becoming an EV superpower. China also aligned its climate objectives with the development of both solar power and EVs to meet net zero targets it set under the Paris climate accord.

It is difficult to argue with a large nation which sets bold targets for decarbonisation and proceeds to accumulate a near monopoly in sourcing of these critical minerals. America, Europe, and rest of the world is playing catch up and over time will make a dent on China's dominance. The data is stunning. *Benchmark Source*[13] estimates that by 2030, the top 10 cobalt-producing countries will account for 96% of the total mined cobalt supply, with just two countries, the DRC and Indonesia, contributing to 84% of total production. Although Chinese firms have a stake in only three out of the top ten cobalt-producing nations, Benchmark estimates that they will own over half of the cobalt production in the DRC and Indonesia as well as 85% of the output from Papua New Guinea. "This will give Chinese companies command of 46% of global cobalt mined supply by 2030, up from 3% in 2023".

It is not good enough for a country to have a near monopoly in sourcing raw material like cobalt and lithium. The country also has to accumulate the technical knowledge and expertise to produce lithium-ion batteries, on which much of the world's EV fleet currently runs. This is where China's Contemporary Amperex Technology Co, or CATL for short, has stepped in to build and supply an estimated one-third of ALL EVs and hybrid vehicles sold globally. CATL is the world's largest battery manufacturer and reported sales of around $40 billion in 2024. CATL competes domestically with car manufacturer BYD, which has also developed expertise in producing batteries. If you examine data from one quarter of 2024 alone, CATL and BYD together accounted for a hefty 52% of global EV battery shipments (with CATL alone accounting for 35%). There are other non-Chinese competitors in the race as well, including Japanese and Korean players like LG and Panasonic.

As early as 2021, American media was fretting about the rising importance of CATL in the EV supply chain. "The battery giant stands as a crucial link in a green-technology chain increasingly dominated by China. Chinese companies, particularly CATL, have secured vast supplies of raw materials that go inside the batteries", *The New York Times* reported,[14] "That dominance has stirred fears in Washington that Detroit could someday be rendered obsolete, and that Beijing could control American driving in the 21st century the way that oil-producing nations sometimes could in the 20th". This has proved to be a huge over-statement because American car manufacturers, prominently Tesla, have acquired a huge slice of the US EV market, building both battery and charging infrastructure in the process. American tariffs against Chinese EV imports also make them uneconomical to be sold there, providing considerable protection for domestic manufacturers.

There is a bigger point of comparison to be made here about the China EV business model – which is built on control of every aspect of the supply chain, including mining of the raw material and battery production – to the leaner approach pursued by Western multinationals in other manufacturing sectors. Apple represents a famous example of a company headquartered in Cupertino, California, which focuses exclusively on design, brand, marketing, and strategy of its smart products, while outsourcing almost every aspect of the production process to outside vendors like Foxconn to build in China and India. Such an approach worked well during the heady years of peak globalisation i.e. until the global financial crisis (GFC) but has suffered considerable pushback over the last two decades. Companies like Apple have been accused of hollowing out America's manufacturing base by relocating production to cheaper wage destinations like China. In the process, China and its work-force employed by Foxconn gained considerable insight and technical knowledge, including mastering the art and science of building sophisticated products at scale. If Apple had decided early on that all of its products should be manufactured in-house and in America, globalisation and cheap wages be damned, it is arguable whether Chinese firms would have retained such a huge manufacturing and technological edge.

Which brings me back to Chinese EVs and consider what its future trajectory is likely to be. A throwaway comment by LSE Professor and Chinese economist Keyu Jin has resonated with me. She told Martin Wolf[15] of the *Financial Times* that the tables have turned when it comes to technology transfers in products like EVs.

> Chinese EV companies, battery companies want to set up shop in Europe and form joint ventures, and there are some mandated technology transfers going the other way, right? Asking the Chinese to transfer

> technology to European companies. So Chinese companies understand that because they think there's a trade-off, access to market. And look, you know you have to give up some. So it's very interesting.

Her point being that Chinese companies are willing to trade their EV or solar production secrets in exchange for market access in Europe. In the interview, Jin also pointed out that when it comes to domestic economy issues, the "China model" is "brilliant at scaling up supply and extremely weak in raising personal demand". The domestic EV industry in China is facing a glut of supply because too many players are competing for market share at a time when the economy is relatively weak and Chinese consumers are holding off on purchases of luxury items like cars. Which is precisely why outsiders fear that without sufficient safeguards, they will be faced with a tidal wave of Chinese EV imports. While the finances of companies like Geely and BYD are sound, there are any number of lower-tier EV makers who are in the red and are on life support.

Here is my proposition to Chinese policymakers, with the realistic assumption that it will not be heard. In mastering the EV supply chain and production, China has demonstrated that it is able to build a global business at scale and secure the brand recognition which is essential for success. However, the implicit and explicit subsidies are going to harm the long-term sustainability of the industry. If BYD or Geely have aspirations to become the Toyota or Ford of this and the next generation, with autonomous EVs representing the next innovation, they will have to learn to compete on a level playing field. Critics will point that I am perhaps being hypocritical in saying this because at the height of the GFC in 2008, the American government did step in to support Detroit car-makers because of their dire financial condition. There is a difference in a government bail-out of a company in trouble, which is typically conditional and temporary, compared with the state offering subsidies and incentives on an ongoing basis. There is a wider question on whether China's aspirations of becoming a fully developed country by 2049, the centenary of the 1949 Communist revolution, will be helped or hindered if its manufacturing sector is riddled with over-capacity and rising costs.

David Halberstam would have appreciated this point. In the Japanese context, he writes in his book that the great surge in the country's economy had come in the 1950s and 1960s, "when a considerable part of its competitive advantage" was due to highly disciplined, inexpensive labour.

> That era was ending, however, as Japan became middle-class.......That meant that there was a serious possibility that the very thing the Japanese had done to the West might now in turn be done to them by their neighbours, countries like Korea or Singapore, where the work-force

was even more disciplined, hungrier, and willing to labour for a good deal less.

Substitute Korea and Singapore with Vietnam, Malaysia, and India and you get the sense that China has limited time in embedding its advanced technology industry at the commanding heights of its economy. Going global, being generous with technology transfers, and remaining competitive will require less state support. It is time for Beijing to allow pure market forces to prevail. Our next chapter, on India's impressive digital stack, offers a way forward.

Notes

1 *The Reckoning*, by David Halberstam, William Morrow & Co, 1986.
2 The quote is from the *Financial Times* – The BYD founder with a battery obsession, March 22, 2025.
3 Xi is making the world pay for China's mistakes – Brad Setser, *The New York Times*, February 18, 2025.
4 China's global electric dominance – Frik Els, April 19, 2024.
5 Prius concept car, Evolution – Toyota Motor Corporation, August 4, 2017.
6 The Strategic Ambiguity of Toyota's EV Play – Alejandro De La Garza, *Time Magazine*, December 4, 2023.
7 How did China dominate electric cars policy –*MIT Technology Review*, February 2021.
8 How China rose to lead the world in electric vehicles, ALJ Insights published by Abdul Latif Jameel, April 17, 2024.
9 Most pricing information is from publicly available sources like car dealers for BYD and Tesla in the UAE.
10 The clip was originally shared on X and my reference is based on an article in India's NDTV World, September 2024.
11 VW Hacked – Did China Steal Their E-Car Secrets – Secure Blink, April 29, 2024.
12 Details of the verdict sourced from law firm MMLC Group's commentary – China Trade Secret Case Sees Record Damages – Geely vs. WM Motor, June 21, 2024.
13 How much cobalt production is owned by Chinese companies – Benchmark Source, October 17, 2024.
14 Why a Chinese company dominates electric car batteries –*The New York Times*, December 22, 2021.
15 Martin Wolf talks to Keyu Jin – Has China's economy run out of gas, *Financial Times*, March 10 2025.

Chapter 7

India

Stack

The improbable story behind the creation of the India Stack, now regarded as world beating digital infrastructure.

As a journalist, which I once was, you keep score of the interesting people you have engaged with during the course of your entire life. In my case, I have not been a working journalist since 1998 but those reporting instincts never go away. I have witnessed the dramatic rise and steep descent of many a business tycoon and political leader. In the Indian context, the two groups listed above are generally a self-absorbed, self-contained lot – disinterested in blending private sector expertise with providing public goods. Moreover, there is little inter-mingling as business leaders seldom stumble into politics and political leaders vice versa, although they do converge due to the confluence of money and power.

Having observed Nandan Nilekani through four-plus decades,[1] first as a journalist in Mumbai in the 1980s when the company he co-founded, Infosys, was a minnow, and much later as an international civil servant, I can say with a great deal of certitude that he stands apart in the crowded space of Indian business and politics. He has achieved the rare trifecta of simultaneously being a billionaire tech tycoon, a politician albeit who lost his electoral race, and a successful technocrat who conceived and delivered the India Stack (IS) – India's world-beating digital infrastructure project that marries the digital identity of the country's 1.4 billion citizens with an interoperable payments and data management system. It may sound like hyperbole but Nilekani and the Indian government's contributions on the IS alone are worthy of a Nobel Peace Prize sometime in the future, so radical it has proven to be in the design and delivery of a citizen's ability to access public services. It is not surprising that the IS model is being widely replicated in many parts of the developing world.

However, we are getting ahead of ourselves and it will be useful to place Nilekani's rise in the wider context of India's economic journey

DOI: 10.4324/9781003603375-10

since 1991, which ushered in economic reforms after several decades of stagnation. To be sure, Nilekani was not *the* founder of Infosys, that credit goes to N.R. Narayana Murthy who founded the company in 1981 and brought together a group of technologists like Nilekani on his mission to build a software services major to rival American software giants like IBM. From an initial business capital of $250, Infosys has grown to become a Nasdaq-listed global IT services player, with revenues of around $20 billion and market capitalisation of $90 billion. Nilekani's own net worth is estimated at $3 billion and he continues to chair the company he co-founded in the early 1980s.

Each one of Nilekani's peer co-founders have also accumulated billions in net worth, with Narayana Murthy having the additional distinction of being the father-in-law of former UK Prime Minister Rishi Sunak. I am emphasising this because like many of his billionaire peers, Nilekani may well have stayed in his lane, a favourite American expression to signify that he could have continued to run Infosys and enjoyed the fruits of the company's remarkable success. Indeed, this is precisely the space occupied by Narayana Murthy and his wife Sudha, who have emerged as authors and public scolds, with the former hectoring Indians to persevere with a punishing 70-hour work week. "If we are not in a position to work hard, then who will work hard", he said as recently as December 2024.[2] Murthy also wants the government to stay out of business. "The government has absolutely no role in entrepreneurship", he said, "I also realised entrepreneurs build a nation as they create jobs, they create wealth for their investors and they pay taxes". Although Murthy is significantly more gentle and tempered when you meet him in person, his recent commentary would not be out of place in Silicon Valley, the land of the tech bro where founders routinely trash the role of government while eagerly lapping up state funding for advanced technology projects.

Nilekani pursued a different path compared to Murthy. His rise or stumble into the public space happened first as an author of *Imagining India,* a successful 2009 work of non-fiction[3] where he articulated many of the ideas that subsequently formed the core of the IS. That book and its ideas caught the attention of Indian Prime Minister Manmohan Singh, a technocrat-turned-politician himself, and in short order Nilekani was tasked with putting his core idea – of giving each one of India's 1.4 billion citizens with a unique digital identity. Nilekani recalls that the notoriously bureaucratic (and prescriptive) Indian government was economical in giving him the mandate to oversee the project. All I had was one page saying, "Give every Indian a unique ID", Nilekani said in a recent interaction[4] with LinkedIn CEO Ryan Roslansky, "It didn't say how...just do it".

To provide him with bureaucratic muscle and political support, Nilekani was appointed Chair of the Unique Identification Authority of India

(UIDAI), a state-owned agency which would originate the technology and coordinate delivery of *Aadhar*,[5] a unique digital identity card which would enable Indians, particularly the country's desperately poor population, to access financial services, receive cash transfers, and capitalise on economic opportunities arising from India's fast growing economy.

To provide some global context on why the UIDAI was such a revolutionary public-private project originating from a developing country like India, America's Big Tech peers like Google (established in 1998) and Meta (established in 2004) were in the same period innovating purely private initiatives in search and social media which enabled these companies to grow in size and wealth over the last few decades. I would argue that Nilekani's *Aadhar* is as influential and powerful as these private sector peers, if not more, in building widely embraced public digital infrastructure. If in private hands and scaled globally, *Aadhar* would have probably been capitalised in the same league as Google's parent, Alphabet and Meta (market cap of $2.45 trillion and $1.96 trillion, respectively, as I write this). The fact that an Indian tech CEO decided that the public infrastructure route was the best way to proceed says a lot about Nilekani and the Indian government at the time.

While the pandemic demonstrated the power of public-private partnerships in developing a vaccine, the *Aadhar* project predated Covid and delivered in a country unfamiliar with such collaborations. Nilekani was able to assemble India's private sector technical talent, relatively easy in a country renowned for its engineering graduates from the IITs and engineering schools.

The project itself, I might add, was improbable and wildly ambitious compared with the ground realities of delivering digital or real public goods in India. This is a sprawling nation where a significant majority of the population, estimated at 69% or 833 million, live in rural areas. The urban India you encounter on travels to New Delhi or Mumbai is a world apart from the rural population, a majority of whom still work as farm labour or in subsistence farming. Although the rates of chronic poverty have plummeted in recent decades, most recent estimates suggest that it has fallen to less than 5%,[6] many parts of rural India still remain inaccessible due to poor transport connectivity and services such as banking. This problem was even more acute when *Aadhar* was launched. For example, the scope of the project was to secure biometrics and retina scans from 1.4 billion people regardless of where they lived. This meant that UIDAI had to establish the distribution infrastructure at the last mile, using the network of rural vendors and small stores, which would allow the state to directly interact with citizens to secure their fingerprints. Since this was also the first time India was embarking on a standardised digital identity exercise, there was the small problem of ensuring that only citizens would be eligible to participate. India does face an illegal immigration challenge on its eastern border with Bangladesh and Myanmar, which the ruling BJP in recent years has drawn political capital from by claiming that the country was being overwhelmed by illegal Muslim migrants. The *Aadhar* project initially faced the daunting task of separating citizens from non-citizens, not an easy task in rural India where few people possessed even a rudimentary form of identity.[7]

The rural biometric and retina scan challenges were particularly acute because the underlying technology had to function robustly in remote areas to allow for accurate data capture. As highlighted in an earlier chapter, India's Election Commission has considerable experience in delivering the electoral apparatus across rural and urban India for several decades. The system is not fool-proof. In rural areas where people have to prove their identity, there are always fears about the integrity of the entire system. *Aadhar* was a game-changer in this regard because in one swoop it was able to provide all Indians with the ability to prove their identity and access services from the state they were eligible to receive, be it welfare benefits or financial services. With the emergence of the smart phone, *Aadhar* also turbocharged a citizen's ability to establish price discovery and to sell their agricultural produce to a different set of intermediaries. Paul Romer, former Chief Economist of the World Bank, was right in praising India's digital identity exercise. "The system in India is the most sophisticated that I've seen", he said, "It's the basis for all kinds of connections that involve things like financial transactions. It could be good for the world if this became widely adopted".

Writing for the Chandler Institute of Governance,[8] Nilekani offers six lessons from *Aadhar* on what makes a digital public infrastructure work at scale. The lessons include absolute minimalism in terms of delivering digital public infrastructure to ensure it "does one thing and only one thing", which in this case was providing a unique identity to 1.4 billion people. There is the second lesson from "building trust by design", where for a digital public infrastructure to work, "every interaction with the infrastructure needs to be trustworthy" – the owners of data have to trust that their data are safe and the users of the data have to believe that every interaction will generate an answer that can be trusted. Nilekani also emphasises the importance of building resilience for failure i.e. systems which function under failure, the importance of not leaving anyone behind, which I illustrated earlier, the need to respect and protect privacy (which we will get to shortly), and what he describes as "distributing the ability to solve". To succeed, he notes that a digital public infrastructure needs an ecosystem of partners that collaborate to enable key components of the project and another set of innovation partners to build upon it to create more value for its recipients.

> *Aadhar* is one of the key components in the creation of the IndiaStack – a set of Application Programming Interfaces (APIs) that allows governments, businesses, startups, and developers to utilise a unique digital identity infrastructure to move India towards presence-less, paperless, and cashless service delivery.

In terms of vision and objective setting, Nilekani's discourse on *Aadhar* is a brilliant exposition of the project's expansive ambitions. While a few critics have dismissed the goals set for the entire project, there are significant concerns about *Aadhar's* failure in data protection and in protecting the underlying infrastructure from cyber-attacks, of which there have been many. Let's dive into these concerns in detail, while also emphasising the positive impacts of the project in driving financial inclusion and preventing spillage in the delivery of welfare benefits. The cyber breaches concerning *Aadhar* and compromises to the digital identities of individuals are very real and scary. In its annual risks report for 2019,[9] the World Economic Forum did not pull its punches concerning the security and safety of the *Aadhar* system. "Malicious cyber-attacks and lax cybersecurity protocols again led to massive breaches of personal information in 2018", the report said, "The largest was in India, where the government ID database, *Aadhar,* reportedly suffered multiple breaches that potentially compromised the records of 1.1 billion registered citizens". The Forum scathingly added that it was reported in January (2018) that "criminals were selling access to the database at a rate of 500 rupees (around $6) for ten minutes, while in March a leak at a state-owned utility company allowed anyone to download names and ID numbers".

In a separate report on the 2018 breach, the Vipre Security Group listed[10] the data at risk from the breach. "They include biometric data, names, physical and email addresses, phone numbers, and the actual 12-digit unique identity numbers of citizens.

> The breach prompted public outcry and legal scrutiny, with activists and privacy advocates highlighting the need for better data protection laws in India. It also influenced decisions around the Supreme Court's decision on the constitutionality of *Aadhar* and its mandatory linking to various services".

Indeed, the Supreme Court ruled in its 2018 judgement that citizens had a fundamental right to privacy and struck down a section of the *Aadhar* Act which enabled private entities to use the system's authentication to establish identity for services. The Court also upheld the constitutionality of the project itself, allowing the government to proceed with its final implementation. Although this has not stopped further issues with the system, a breach on the scale of 2018 has not been repeated. Before we direct our ire against Nilekani for flawed security, I must emphasise that he has not been in charge of UIDAI since Prime Minister Modi swept into power in 2014. After hesitating on whether to pursue the digital identity project which it inherited from the previous government, the ruling BJP embraced *Aadhar* and has extracted political capital from it. Prime Minister Modi in 2017[11] declared that the project has added great strength to India's development. "What would earlier get into the wrong hands is now going to the intended beneficiaries", he said, referring to the project's ability to directly help recipients of welfare benefits.

The transformational nature of *Aadhar* is one reason why India's digital identity project is proving to be a role model for other developing nations – it has been relatively cost-effective to develop and deliver compared with similar systems in the developed world. Researchers at Yale University estimate that the initial project costs (of securing the biometric identity of all citizens) around $10 per person (some other estimates I have seen are as less as $1 per person). Which means that the initial project cost worked out to a modest $10–12 billion, affordable for a large developing country with limited resources. "It was very, very cost effective because it was done using a decentralised approach leveraging local resources without creating a large bureaucratic infrastructure, which is normally the way most things in India get done", the Yale researchers noted.[12] Although the registration process for the *Aadhar* card was voluntary, there was an incentive for citizens to do so because it was explicitly linked with access to welfare benefits. *Aadhar's* designers, the Yale study points out, had to create a system that could scale up quickly while ensuring no duplication or fraud. "When you're at 1000 people or even a million people in the system, that is easy", Yale Professor Sudhir says

> But when you started getting 600 million people in your data base, with each new entry added you need to compare the entry against every one of the 600 million people already in the system for duplication, that is very computationally challenging.

The solution provided by Nilekani and team was to create a "very simple and cheap front end" for data collection of the fingerprints and registration that was easy for people to access close to their homes, but a "very sophisticated back-end infrastructure that ensured data integrity". The last bit is of course contentious as I highlighted earlier.

India stands out even compared with the developed world in its ability to build a national digital identity system at scale and within a reasonable cost envelop. As a point of comparison, the UK in the early 2000s flirted with the idea of delivering a distinctive national identity card to all citizens and the project was mired in cost-overruns and controversy. Here is *The Guardian*[13] explaining what went wrong. In 2007, after several years of project cost escalations, the official cost of delivering ID cards to the country's then 60 million population was estimated at around £6 billion. "The government says it has yet to fix the price of the ID card, but the average cost would be £93 combined with the passport, and ministers intend the scheme to be self-financing", the newspaper reported. The project was eventually scrapped but it is still helpful to compare the UK's fraught experience with that of India. With a population less than the western Indian state of Gujarat (72 million) and per-capita income significantly higher than that of India, costs in the UK were always going to be higher. India also enjoyed the benefits of scale from a larger population. Yet it must be said that managing and delivering large public-private projects in India carry significantly higher risks and the fact that *Aadhar* was delivered on a relatively frugal budget and on time is testimony to the success of the venture.

Not surprisingly, many developing countries have been queuing up before Indian policymakers to learn and adapt *Aadhar* to their specific circumstances. The World Bank has provided a platform in the form of the Identification for Development Initiative (ID4D) and has used the *Aadhar* project as a foundational case study in advising other developing countries to roll out digital national identity programs. In its most recent annual report[14] (2023), the ID4D notes that it is on track to "improve the lives of 550 million people in nearly 60 countries by 2025". The initiative aims to enable people to access ID that "empowers them through increased access to services and economic opportunities, and greater ability to access their rights". Having spent a considerable amount of time in the multilateral economic space, the south-south transfer of knowledge and skills, as represented by *Aadhar* and many other initiatives, is a refreshing development.

As we discussed in a previous chapter, the developed world had a monopoly over the transmission of knowledge and skills for much of the seven decades since World War II. There was a strong, underlying belief that reverse flows of knowledge were simply not feasible because of the relative levels of knowledge and sophistication between the developed and developing countries. *Aadhar,* along with other home-grown technology-driven initiatives such as MPESA, the radical mobile money transfer project in Kenya, has emboldened developing countries to look south and east for ideas, skills, and knowledge transfers. Some have even dared to suggest that the developed west should be open to innovations originating from developing countries.

As a complete aside, within a few weeks of arriving in Washington D.C. in July 1998 to work for the IMF, I was amused with a report in *The Wall Street Journal,*[15] which declared that the World Bank, "having wrestled with poverty, decay, and mismanagement from Bombay to Brazzaville, is now taking on the economic development woes of Washington D.C.". At that time, the nation's capital (which hosts both the IMF and the World Bank) was emerging from a dark period of high crime, drug abuse, and decay in public infrastructure and services. The Bank's President at the time, James Wolfensohn, offered the District of Columbia, which runs the capital its international staff expertise in a range of public policy areas it typically provided to developing countries – such as health, education, and infrastructure. It is not clear if the offer was ever taken up but it illustrates that globally applicable good ideas today can simply originate from any part of the world. In the Indian context, it certainly has with the IS.

What is the IS and how is it different from *Aadhar*? A simple way of explaining it is that biometric identification is the foundation on which the Indian government built a super app that would revolutionise payments, drive financial inclusion, empower the poor, and prevent massive corruption in the country's welfare system. Here is Nilekani explaining[16] the transformative nature of the IS. "We think this model is unique, its collaborative, it's equitable, and it's based on the principle that opportunity must be made available to everyone in the country, irrespective where they are". Let me give you an on-the-ground illustration of how the IS actually translates into on-the-ground impact. I am a frequent visitor to Mumbai, India's commercial capital, and vividly recall that I had to carry around large quantities of cash as recently as a decade ago for a simple reason. India was primarily a cash society, and daily transactions with a road-side vendor or a taxi driver had to be settled in wads of rupee notes. That reality has changed dramatically as anyone visiting India these days can attest. The three-wheeler cab operator in suburban Mumbai has a sign in his tiny vehicle announcing that he accepts digital payments. Ditto the road-side vendor selling fruits and vegetables, and I am not stretching the truth that even the neighbourhood beggar, armed with multiple cell-phones, has the capability to accept donations via Google Pay or Paytm, two of the country's largest digital payment providers. The sad reality, at least for me, is that I still have to carry around large quantities of cash because I don't have access to the domestic payment rails. When I offer my American or British credit cards for payment, the same three-wheeler driver who regarded cash as king a decade ago now rolls his eyes and asks. "You don't have Google Pay?" is the usual question thrown at me, with a mixture of astonishment and disdain. I have to swallow my pride and offer rupee notes and witness the astonishing development that the driver does not carry much cash and insists that I give him the precise amount.

This revolution in payments was made possible with the Indian government's decision in 2014 to launch JAM. In a nutshell, JAM stands for three critical elements of the identity, inclusion, payments, and benefits ecosystem. The J stands for *Jan Dhan*, roughly translated as public money or wealth; the A stands for *Aadhar*, the digital identification platform; and the M stands for the mobile phone. Put together, the JAM scheme's early ambition was to leverage on the fact that over 1 billion Indians possessed a unique digital identity, which was then turbocharged by the state opening bank accounts for those who were under-banked, and to build smartphone-enabled national payments infrastructure which would enable almost every Indian to transact and make and receive payments. Prime Minister Modi, who loves lofty rhetoric and the turn of the phrase, declared at JAM's launch in 2014 that for him, JAM stood for "Just Achieving Maximum", which he went on to explain meant – maximum value for every rupee spent, maximum empowerment for our poor, and maximum technology penetration among the masses. The rhetoric aside, on each one of these metrics, India has achieved critical mass in the identity and payments space.

There are gaps and vulnerabilities of course and I don't want to paint a uniformly positive picture. I will use two metrics to assess the impact of the JAM scheme. The first metric is digital payments with Google Pay as an interesting case study and the second is direct benefit transfers (DBTs), which the state is using to directly remit welfare payments to the poor. Google Pay, along with multiple state-owned and purely private players utilise UPI, the universal payments interface, developed and managed by the National Payments Corporations of India (NPCI), which is owned by the government. It is the UPI interface which enables my neighbourhood fruit vendor and three-wheeler driver to accept digital payments and to scorn at less privileged foreigners. While Google Pay has struggled to make inroads in its home market, America, the payments app had a hefty 35% market share of all UPI payments made in India in 2023.

> While Google has aggressive domestic competitors in India's payments space like the Walmart-backed Phone Pe and local fintech giant Paytm and has been accused of monopolistic practices given the dominance of its app store, the US tech juggernaut has nevertheless mostly avoided regulatory travails in the subcontinent.

Forbes magazine[17] noted, "That is because in India's fintech market, Google is a global company that usually manages to think locally".

It is a mutually beneficial arrangement between Google and the Indian government. The fact that a major global player has a dominant share of the Indian digital payments market is a proof point for the government that it is welcoming to foreign investors. The presence of Google and other international names also enables the government to showcase the impact of UPI at home and its easy applicability in other developing countries. One example of this is the NPCI's agreement with its counterpart in Singapore to facilitate real-time money transfers, a contentious and walled-off space which used to make it prohibitively expensive for Indian workers in the city-state and elsewhere, for example, to remit their income home. "We are also excited about enabling a seamless and more connected international remittance network by further expanding UPI's cross-border interoperability feature", an NPCI official said,[18] referring to the partnership with Google Pay, "With the success of the UPI in a dynamic market like India we are excited to further our vision to transform the digital payments landscape globally".

In many ways, the evolving Google-Indian government partnership, particularly in third countries, is a model for how Big Tech companies should operate in developing countries. Usually regarded as companies with a winner-take-all predatory approach to doing business, the Indian example demonstrates that public-private partnerships can work at global scale. The same principle can be applied to developing countries eager to learn from India's experience in DBTs, the process of directly transferring welfare payments to the bank accounts of the poor. This has never been easy in India and indeed in vast swathes of the developing world. The process of fiscal transfers to the poor has traditionally been leaky i.e. middle-men and intermediaries have swallowed a significant portion of the proceeds before it reaches the beneficiary, if at all. Instead of cash, many countries, Brazil notably, have experimented with payments in kind with strings attached. Under Brazil's *Bolsa Familia* welfare program, for example, poor families receive conditional cash transfers (CCTs) on the condition that their children attend school and carry out mandatory health checks. I am grossly simplifying the design and intent of the program but it is regarded as a model social welfare program because it conditions cash transfers on recipient families agreeing to carry out health and education pre-conditions before the money reaches the head of the family, who is the mother.

Under India's DBT, government data show that it has been used under 310 official social welfare schemes across 53 different organs of the state. Researcher Shamika Ravi estimates that the DBT has resulted in annual savings of around 1.14% of India's GDP, meaningful because it amounts to around $42 billion. "DBT preserves the dignity of the poor", she writes,[19] "Even though dignity might be challenging to quantify, it should be recognised that even without corruption and leakages, the poor would have to undertake a poverty parade to avail government benefits". This change in approach, she argues, where instead of the poor availing of government benefits, it's the government benefits that reach them without an intermediary, has important implications for their "psyche".

Market libertarians scoff at cash transfers and welfare benefits over ideological grounds that a nanny state is unduly interfering in the lives of citizens. However, as both *Bolsa Familia* and *Aadhar* have shown, social transformation in large, complex societies like Brazil and India cannot happen without state intervention. Such intervention has benign characteristics, as *Aadhar* has shown, and entirely malign ones as well, as the leakage of fiscal transfers in the past proves. Technology has proven to be a powerful bridge to flatten the hierarchy and empower the poor to access welfare benefits and more generally to integrate with the modern economy (as my road-side vendor has done). Warts and all, Nandan Nilekani's germ of a digital idea in 2009 has flowered into the country's digital revolution. We turn next to another adventurer in a different country on a different continent – Nigeria, Africa, to examine what it took to build an oil refinery from scratch.

Notes

1 To be sure, I did not approach or speak with Nilekani on this chapter, using interviews with other sources and publicly available information.
2 These quotes of Narayana Murthy have been taken from a report in ITPro, December 17, 2024.
3 *Imagining India – The Idea of a Renewed Nation–* by Nandan Nilekani, Penguin Books India, 2009.
4 The quote is from an article in Business Today, December 1, 2024.
5 In Sanskrit and Hindi, Aadhar roughly translates into base or foundation.
6 Data from Forbes India, March 5, 2025 – Poverty rate in India (2024). Trend over the years and causes.
7 The project subsequently delinked the enrolment in Aadhar from a person's nationality, ensuring that the process of gaining digital identity does not confer any rights or benefits. Source – A decade of UIDAI: Challenge and Impact – Startup Talky, October 10, 2020.
8 India's Aadhar System: Bringing E-Government to Life – Nandan Nilekani, Chandler Institute of Governance. No date cited.
9 World Economic Forum – The Global Risks Report 2019.
10 Vipre Security Group – Digital Disasters: The Biggest Data Breaches of All Time – March 13, 2024.
11 The quote is from a report in The Wire – Modi took a 180-degree turn on Aadhar, May 22, 2024.
12 What happens when a billion identities are digitized – Yale Insights, March 17, 2020.
13 *The Guardian* – Costs of national ID card scheme soars by £840 m in six months – May 10, 2007.
14 World Bank, ID4D, 2023 annual report – Putting people at the centre of digital public infrastructure.

15 The World Bank Aids Washington As It Does Third-World Nations –*The Wall Street Journal*, August 27, 1998.
16 India achieved in 9 years what would have taken 47 years by traditional means –*Business Today*, August 7, 2023.
17 India's UPI gets a boost in its quest to go global –*Forbes*, January 19, 2024.
18 India payments body links up with Google Pay to "propel UPI onto global stage" – Global Government Fintech, January 18, 2024.
19 For government schemes, a path to dignity for the poor – Shamika Ravi, *Indian Express*, November 28, 2023.

Chapter 8

Nigeria

Refinery

For the sceptics, Aliko Dangote's bold plan to build a massive oil refinery in Nigeria was a foolhardy venture. How did he prove them wrong?

Why Nigeria? Let me address this question straightaway because the west African country, to put it politely, has an image problem. In the investing world, it falls under the category of a "frontier" market, not quite emerging and surely not emerged. However, Nigeria and the refinery case study I am about to present aligns well with the theme of the book – that there are case studies of excellence in the emerged and even the frontier world that deserve the world's attention. Which is why I selected Nigeria and an astonishing case study of how an oil refinery was conceived and built.

Let me digress first and turn to one of my favourite movies. In German director Werner Herzog's masterful 1982 movie *Fitzcarraldo,* the Irish protagonist wants to transport an entire steamship across the Andean mountains in Peru to profit from a rubber venture. The Irishman also has a fever dream to use the proceeds to build an opera house literally in the middle of nowhere in Peru. The movie powerfully documents human hubris, and for movie buffs of a certain age, *Fitzcarraldo* has become shorthand for human follies past and present. Let me also add that the movie documents the fictional character turning mad during the process of implementing his dream project and Klaus Kinski, the actor who portrayed him also suffered a nervous breakdown while shooting the movie.

It is in this context that I would like to introduce Aliko Dangote, Nigeria and Africa's richest tycoon with interests in cement, sugar, fertiliser, salt, oil & gas, and port infrastructure. The group is Africa's largest cement producer, employs over 30,000 people, and reported revenues of around $5 billion last year. "Dangote's repeated bets on the rise of Africa's middle class helped him amass a fortune from cement, sugar, salt, and other commodities, resulting in a net worth of $28 billion, nearly double that of the second-richest African", *The Wall Street Journal* reported[1] in early 2025.

DOI: 10.4324/9781003603375-11

CEO Today[2] is even more effusive when describing the tycoon. "Dangote's success is a testament to his entrepreneurial spirit, resilience, and foresight" according to the magazine

> Yet his journey is about more than wealth accumulation – it's a story of creating opportunities, driving innovation, and inspiring a continent. From humble beginnings in Kano, Nigeria, to leading one of Africa's most diversified conglomerates, Dangote's story is an inspiring blueprint for aspiring entrepreneurs worldwide.

Dangote, whose foundation has an extensive charitable footprint, also aspires of becoming known as "Africa's Rockefeller", after the American tycoon of the early 20th century who was renowned for business acumen and charitable endeavours which are still flourishing.

To come to *Fitzcarraldo,* I must emphasise that the African tycoon's travails proved to be less fatal than the fictional Irishman featured in the movie and also did not suffer the fate of the actor who portrayed him. But his ambition of building one of the world's largest oil refineries eminently qualifies him to feature in a Werner Herzog movie. When the 68-year Dangote announced plans to build Africa's largest oil refinery in 2016, that too in Nigeria, he was scorned and laughed at. The legion of sceptics and second-guessers publicly and privately derided the plan and described it as "Dangote's folly", a project which would consume time, attention, resources but would eventually fall short. They were worries that Dangote was "biting off more than he could chew", in the words put to me by a London banker in 2016 when the project was conceived, and it would undermine the group's other, more profitable operations. Before I dive deep into the refinery's pathway, another digression is needed to describe Aliko Dangote and Nigeria, the country where he was born and built his commanding empire. The story is incomplete without understanding both.

Ground Zero of this expedition is surely Lagos, the country's commercial capital and the epicentre of the country's exuberant chaos and dysfunction. Having been raised in India and worked in Mumbai in the 1980s, I am used to the maniacal momentum of big cities in developing countries. They have a language and rhythm of their own and what looks like anarchy to an outsider is actually modern capitalism at work. However, even jaded me was stunned after landing in Lagos. I had spent the previous 48 hours in Abuja, the country's capital to the north, which can politely be described as a violent mishmash of architecture styles and the city lacked soul. In Lagos, it is all soul and the street view, in as much as there are one, is a giant laboratory of entrepreneurship and enterprise. I passed through a district which apparently specialised in retrofitting used cars and spare parts and it was a sight to behold. This was micro entrepreneurship at work, as young men agitated for attention and market share. Their moves were carefully choreographed, as though for a ballet dancer, with the exception being that the balletic moves by young men were designed to avoid potholes and petty extortion from the state, which is an unfortunate reality in Nigeria. There is the other glittery side to Lagos too, centred on Victoria Island, home to Ferrari dealerships, large villas with manicured lawns, and pricey restaurants which would not be out of place in Dubai or Singapore.

The overwhelming message that a visitor gets in Lagos, and it may well be true of what residents are hearing too, is this – you are on your own, the state is awol, and make what you can of the opportunities presented to you. This is because Nigeria is an intriguing combination of the wild west and wilder east. Nigeria's politics since independence has been equally combustible with a bloody civil war in the 1960s, successive Army coups, and a semblance of democracy since 1999. As Leena Koni Hoffman and Jon Wallace, Associate Fellows at Chatham House, noted[3] in 2022, Nigeria's democracy has been fragile and fluctuating since independence.

> Successive governments have struggled to create a sense of national unity in a complex country whose borders were drawn up by British colonialists, incorporating more than 200 ethnic groups. Democratization and development have progressed at different speeds in the country's disparate regions.

For good measure, they added that Nigeria's democracy has had a "long and troubled relationship" with its military. "For almost half of its existence as an independent state, Nigeria has been under military rule instead of civilian administration". The country's political system has parallels with both Pakistan (generals meddling in politics) and Venezuela (oil being the primary source of revenue, pillage, and patronage).

Given the messy politics, there are obvious negative spillovers on the economic front as well. Nigeria may be one of the world's largest producers of oil and gas, with proven reserves estimated to be the tenth largest in the world, but that has not translated into economic growth and opportunity for the country's 227 million citizens. The country has a per capita GDP of just over $2,000 and the industrial base is hollow. At a restaurant in one of Lagos' swishy five-star hotels, a Nigerian friend remarked to me that even the serviettes placed on the bar counter were imported. Nigeria in many ways epitomises the "resource curse", where the country's overwhelming dependence on oil revenues and imports of basic staples has established a system rife in rent extraction and crony capitalism.

"For decades, Nigeria's economy has been defined by a paradox: a nation rich in resources yet crippled by import dependency", writes Oluyemi Adeosun.[4]

> Despite vast oil wealth, fertile lands, entrepreneurial population, the country remains a net importer of everything from refined petroleum to basic food items. This unsustainable model drains foreign reserves, weakens the naira,[5] and leaves the economy vulnerable to global shocks.

He added that "change is possible", with strategic industrial policies, a shift in value chain positioning, and urgent fixes to infrastructure bottlenecks. The Borgen Project says[6] that Nigeria also ranked 150th out of the 157 countries in the World Bank's 2020 Human Capital Index, indicating a lack of adequate living standards from poor opportunities in education and healthcare to ensure a productive labour force. "These indicators of poverty relate to the neglect of other industries that come from the resource curse and the lack of economic diversification to provide adequate socio-economic opportunities for Nigerians to escape poverty".

All in all, this volatile backdrop is not exactly the breeding ground for an entrepreneur determined to reduce import dependence and to build an industrial base. Lest the previous paragraphs present a uniformly negative picture about Nigeria, let me reiterate that despite considerable odds, the country is fertile breeding ground for entrepreneurship and talent. The talent is visible in Nigeria's global music stars like Burna Boy and Remi, in writers like Chimamanda Ngozi Adichie, and of course business tycoons like Aliko Dangote. Although he was born and raised in northern Nigeria and is a practising Muslim (unlike residents of Lagos, which skews heavily Christian), it was here that Aliko Dangote decided to establish his first business in the late 1970s – in the trading and imports of cement. Like everything else in Nigeria's economy, the country was a major importer of cement and Dangote's ambition was to supplant import dependence by the building of one of Africa's largest manufacturing facilities.

"When Aliko Dangote was building his business running four cement trucks in Nigeria in the late 1970s, a relative gave him $750,000 to expand", Alvin Powell of *The Harvard Gazette*[7] writes, "Business was booming – there was a cement shortage – but instead of investing the money in the businesses, he gave it back". Dangote's response as he recounted this story many years later. "I was scared, as a small entrepreneur to lose his money. So, I returned it back to him".

A research paper[8] on Dangote Cement, published by the African Studies Centre in Leiden, the Netherlands, chronicles the political and business fault lines which Dangote had to navigate to build his cement empire.

It acknowledges upfront that doing business in Nigeria requires business savvy and good relations with the state.

> Although Dangote Cement is a beneficiary of the complex state-business relations in Nigeria, this alone cannot fully explain the phenomenal success of the company. In addition to Aliko Dangote's close association with the government, his entrepreneurial skills have also played an important part in this success story.

The research paper goes on to argue that the success of Dangote Cement was "greatly assisted" by the ability of the tycoon to understand the dynamics of the Nigerian business and political environment. "This aided in the timing of his investment decision that enabled Dangote Cement to transform from a cement importer to a cement manufacturer in Nigeria", the paper notes. Market timing also helped, as cement demand in Nigeria soared by a phenomenal 400% between 2000 and 2014 from a modest 5.62 million tonnes to 23 million metric tonnes. Dangote "exploited" this demand to rapidly increase cement production capacity from 900,000 tonnes in 2000 to 28.2 million tonnes in 2014. Production capacity has since soared to 52 million tonnes across ten countries in sub-Saharan Africa, making Dangote Cement the continent's biggest cement manufacturers and one of its most valuable companies.

Dangote does not romanticise or underplay the challenges of doing business in Nigeria and the wider continent. "Investing in Africa is not easy. It's very profitable, but very challenging", he told *The Harvard Gazette*. For years, Dangote said, he would go into work dreading the unanticipated problems he was "sure" to face. But he eventually made his peace with them, realising that such problems came with the territory and that he'd deal with each in its time, rather than fretting about them even before they even arrived. "I developed a thick skin. In the environment where we operate, there will be problems every single day", he said.

This thick skin has enabled Dangote and his cement-led conglomerate to dominate the market in Nigeria and other large markets where it operates. While the continent lags other regions in cement consumption per capita, the remarkable aspect of Africa is that it still has considerable way to go in terms of scaling demand. According to another research paper[9] published in 2023, the macro case for cement is compelling. Sub-Saharan Africa is currently home to over 1.1 billion people, and the United Nations estimates that by 2050, the region will have a population of more than 2.1 billion and two-thirds of this will be absorbed by urban areas, which will be home to an additional 950 million people.

> The Global Infrastructure Hub (G20) estimates that $2.4 trillion will be needed as investment to bring Africa's standard up to the global

> standard. As a result, Africa will be in urgent need of more infrastructure, housing, and commercial buildings as the population expands.

The company is facing headwinds on two fronts. First, Chinese and other global cement manufacturers attempt to capture market share in Nigeria and across the continent. Chinese cement producers are being closely watched because of their ability to swamp the market with supply and continuing concerns about the level of state subsidies the firms receive, as we discussed in the previous chapter on electric vehicles (EVs).

> The Chinese can also be very aggressive when they get into any market: they also typically get state backing from their country for most of their investments. They are likely to come with even more resources to strengthen their competitive position.

Muda Yusuf of the Centre for the Promotion of Private Enterprises told *The Africa Report.*[10] This underscores that competition from China's more nimble manufacturers is casting a long shadow even in Africa, and this does raise concerns over domestic economic resilience and adverse impact on entrepreneurship. If everything in Africa's marketplace is made in China, as is already the case in both low-tech (textiles, crockery, toys, trinkets) and medium- and high-tech manufacturing (cement being one example), concerns about a hollowing out of the continent's already brittle manufacturing base are not farfetched. Moreover, with most of the continent's population under the age of 30, Africa needs to create millions of manufacturing jobs to keep pace with the millions of young men and women entering the job market each year. On his part, Dangote is investing heavily in training employees and in skills development for youth through his foundation, which has been described as the continent's largest private endowment.

The second headwind faced by the group originates from its primary product – cement, which is amongst the most polluting substances in the world and contributes significantly to global warming. *Scientific American*[11] does not mince words when describing its particularly polluting characteristics. "Cement – the powdery binder that holds the sand or crushed stone in concrete together – is one the most energy intensive products on the planet", the magazine declared, "Limestone used in is baked at up to 1,450 degrees Celsius (2,640 degrees Fahrenheit) in enormous kilns that are fired almost exclusively with fossil fuels. The chemical reactions involved produce even more carbon dioxide as a by-product". The magazine added that making 1 kg of cement sends 1 kg of CO_2 into the atmosphere. Worldwide every year cement and concrete production generates as much as 9% of all human CO_2 emissions.

Not surprisingly, cement production has been at the crosshairs of global climate activists and governments in their efforts to curb emissions and combat global warming. This raises a troubling philosophical and moral question about whether a poor continent like Africa should be following more developed regions in curbing cement production and consumption. As things stand, Africa only contributes around 4% to global carbon emissions and the continent is in desperate need of sustained growth, where cement is an essential enabler.

In my previous book, *The Notorious ESG*,[12] I had put this question to V. Shankar, a director of Dangote Industries and co-founder and CEO of Gateway Partners,[13] a private equity fund domiciled in Dubai and Singapore. "One could argue that if cement were a country, it would be the third or fourth largest polluter in the world and therefore you should cease all production", he said

> But cement is a fundamental pillar of development. Should we say that Africans should not have cement and live in thatched huts. Or should we only use green cement which is going to cost multiple times as much as the traditional product? The answer is Africans need access to as much cement as they need because they are only now starting off on their development journey.

He added that there was a need to balance and nuance the trade-offs between job security, food, development, and simultaneously tackling the climate challenge.

On its part, Dangote Cement acknowledges the contribution of cement to global warming and is taking steps to decarbonise its operations, albeit at a different timeline compared with global cement majors operating in developed markets. Arvind Pathak, the Managing Director of Dangote Cement, told a cement industry conference in 2023[14] that the company is one of the "pioneer" African companies in decreasing CO2 emissions through a fuel substitution strategy. The alternative fuels for cement production being considered are the use of municipal, agricultural, and industrial wastes. To be sure, Dangote Cement and its peers are a long way off in manufacturing so-called green cement at scale.

If Dangote's cement is proving to be a contentious product in the global warming debate, Aliko's decision in 2016 to establish the continent's largest oil refinery in Nigeria is even more controversial. This is because of fossil fuels, particularly crude and refined oil's primacy in contributing to global emissions. The African context is equally important to consider – while the continent's is amongst the biggest oil producers in the world (with Nigeria, Angola, Libya, Algeria, and Egypt topping production of around 10 million barrels per day), the continent is also the world's poorest with the largest concentration of low-income countries. The typical African policymaker's preoccupation is not to curb global emissions – as is the case with his counterparts in the developed world. The African policymaker's worries include how to make ends meet with soaring deficits and declining revenues and to build the engine of economic growth. It is this calculus which motivated Aliko to embark on his oil refinery project, betting that Nigeria's status as an exporter of crude oil rather than that of value-added refined products was a compelling enough business case. It was also common sense because Nigeria was exporting all its crude and importing some of it back as refined products, exacerbating the country's balance of payments. Aliko's ambition was to build Africa's largest refinery with a capacity to process 650,000 barrels of crude oil per day, which will be a significant improvement in dollar savings as Nigeria's current crude production is around 2 million barrels per day. In 2021 alone, Nigeria imported an estimated $43 billion in petroleum products, placing tremendous pressure on its balance of payments. There is something strange about the resource curse which seems to prevent countries rich in oil from developing downstream and value-added refinery capacity. I witnessed the same phenomenon in Indonesia over three decades ago when the country struggled to build refining capacity, which resulted in importing vast quantities from neighbouring Singapore.

The Dangote project would eventually consume $23 billion in investment and create a virtual industry of naysayers who proclaimed that it would never be built. Its adjacent petrochemicals complex has an annual production capacity of 3 million tonnes of urea, making it Africa's largest fertiliser producer. The only comparator in the developing world for Aliko's refinery ambitions is the massive Reliance Industries refinery at Jamnagar, India, which currently processes over 1.2 million bpd and *is* the world's largest oil refinery. Amit Jain of CNBC Africa believes that both Aliko and Reliance Chair Mukesh Ambani have a lot in common. "Both men have made their fortunes in heavily regulated markets. Both have benefitted from protectionist industrial policies", he writes,[15] "They have been accused of political patronage and they both have a reputation for making bold investments. It is also a remarkable coincidence that they have both thrived in unequal societies". This comment is a tad unfair because the same point could be made about any number of US tech billionaires who are similarly thriving from political patronage in a hugely unequal society.

While all these comments are more recent, after the refinery was commissioned, even Aliko perhaps did not factor in the risks and obstruction he would face in getting the project off the ground, particularly at home. The point should be made that Elon Musk, business genius that he might be, would probably have given up against the odds of setting up a major business in Nigeria. For those unfamiliar with Nigeria's "crude" oil politics, here is a short primer. First, in its oil production belt in southern Nigeria, centred around Rivers State and the Niger Delta (just east of Lagos), Nigeria faces the fundamental problem of oil gangsters, to put it politely, who for decades have illegally siphoned oil from the pipeline and sold it on in a thriving black market, depriving the state of billions in revenue. A report in *Al Jazeera*[16] estimated that in 2022 alone, Nigeria lost an estimated $22 billion in revenue from oil theft and pipeline vandalism. The modus operandi of these oil gangsters is to siphon oil from deliberately ruptured pipelines and sell the proceeds to foreign smugglers, who are willing to pay a modest premium for getting the crude oil into international markets. To be sure, oil theft has been a perennial problem unlikely to be resolved by the commissioning of the Dangote refinery. However, it illustrates the extent of the country's misgovernance of natural resources and inability for the state to combat theft and smuggling.

The second problem is even more pernicious but ultimately resolvable through sound fiscal policies. The Nigerian government, like many other resource rich nations, heavily subsidises the consumer price for finished petroleum products i.e. what consumers pay at the gas station. As imports of refined products soared, Nigeria became a hostage to wild swings in global oil markets. As Amit Jain explains, as the country's imports soared, the state decided to subsidise importers, the middlemen who profited from the trade, by capping the price of gasoline at the retail pump and compensating importers for the difference between the landed cost of oil and pump prices. These subsidies touch a peak of $7 billion a few years ago and have gradually been reduced (an estimated $3.7 billion in 2024 alone) as the state comes to grips with a fiscal and foreign exchange crisis. "It is a burden the government has been trying to get rid of for years but with little success", Jain writes in the same article, "A cosy nexus of politicians, traders, union leaders, and petrol smugglers have benefitted enormously from this knotty problem, and they have tried to keep things the way they are".

Aliko Dangote's business plan to build an oil refinery went beyond economics and struck at the heart of Nigerian elites who profited handsomely over the years from state subsidies. "I knew there would be a fight", he said at an investment conference[17] in June 2024, "But I didn't know that the mafia in oil, they are stronger than the mafia in drugs". There were acts of sabotage during the refinery construction phase, and Aliko had to simultaneously wrestle with domestic opposition and foreign sceptics. The actual civil engineering construction process also proved to be formidable. "It took 18 months to prepare the land for the project", *The Wall Street Journal* reported, "Then the land had to be raised nearly 5 feet to protect it from a rising ocean, which required the equivalent of 6.5 million truckloads of sand, dredged from offshore so as not to disturb local fish populations". Aliko also had to purchase 320 cranes and poured 75 miles of concrete inside the refinery. He also had enough electrical cabling "to encircle the earth twice".

Nearly 11 years after the project was originally conceived, the Dangote refinery was finally commissioned with much fanfare in 2024. "This is a very, very big relief", he told *Forbes Africa*,[18] "It is actually removing something off my chest. Because nobody ever gave us a chance to prove this through". Not so fast, said Nigeria's newly appointed President Bola Tinubu's government which came to power in 2023 and set off a new round of recrimination and investigation. In summary, Aliko faced fierce local opposition to secure an agreement with the state-owned oil company to start refining crude, saving the country precious foreign exchange. Predictably, there were raids on Dangote headquarters by state tax inspectors and unspecified tax evasion charges were threatened as negotiations with the oil company reached a deadlock. All these issues appear to be satisfactorily resolved in Dangote's favour as the refinery, as of writing this chapter, has started refining crude oil and threats of tax investigations have abated somewhat.

I hope readers are now convinced why I decided to profile Aliko Dangote and his ill-fated refinery project, at least during the construction phase. The comparison with Elon Musk, also African born, is very relevant. Western media is awestruck by a tycoon like Musk, who has beaten technological rather than primal political odds like Aliko and succeeded in building a much-admired business in EVs, solar, space exploration, and social media. Business tycoons from the emerged world featured in international media, almost all of it headquartered in America or Europe, have had more unkind things said about them. Their success, for example, is overwhelmingly attributed to political connections and crony capitalism. Both are essential features of doing business in less developed markets, I acknowledge. However, the most remarkable transformation over the past two decades has been the unholy alliance between big business and politics in America. Academic Robert Reich has described[19] this phenomenon as "super capitalism" and has authored two books on the topic. His primary thesis is that there is heavy income concentration in America, and consequently political power has also become too concentrated in the hands of too few.

Since Reich's books were published in 2008 and 2016, there has been an even more contentious debate in America on the merits of "woke" capitalism – which can loosely be described as a set of policies pursued by C-suites, often under investor or societal pressure, to reduce emissions and to strengthen diversity and inclusion. It is richly ironic to see America's corporate titans buckle under political pressure and shelve many of the central tenets of stakeholder capitalism aka currently derided as being too "woke". While large American corporations are becoming nervous about advocating for greater equality in the workplace and to combat global warming, the baton in many ways has passed on to emerged world tycoons like Aliko Dangote and Nandan Nilekani. With one exception as I note below.

Dangote's ambition of becoming known as the "Rockefeller of Africa" rests on widely praised philanthropy initiatives as well as a recognition that cement and crude oil are major polluters, and the group needs to innovate to reduce emissions from the production process. Fresh from his success in establishing *Aadhar,* Nandan Nilekani has established the EkStep (which translates to one step) Foundation in India, whose core objective (amongst many) is to use technology as an enabler to widen access to learning opportunities and quality jobs. This is a particularly pressing issue in India because of the country's demographic dividend and abundant surplus of young people.

Now for the exception. Both Dangote and Nilekani, like many other tycoons in the emerged world, are emulating Microsoft founder Bill Gates who has now pledged to donate the rest of his wealth, estimated at a staggering $200 billion, for health and education initiatives worldwide and to shut his eponymous foundation at the end of 2045. Since most of the Trump administration's recent budget cuts have centred around Africa, with the shuttering of USAID and allied aid initiatives, philanthropic initiatives like Gates's and Dangote hold out a more positive outlook for the continent. Gates himself, responding to a question on whether the "moral math" (to support low-income and vulnerable countries) was inarguable, noted that there was an underlying logic for stepping up rather than scaling down assistance. "I think there's a logic to solving tuberculosis", he said in an interview,[20] "I mean, its criminal not to solve H.I.V. It's criminal not to eradicate malaria". In the absence of Western aid and philanthropic benevolence, countries across the emerged and frontier world must take away the central message that Aliko Dangote and his Nigerian compatriots have known for several decades – they are on their own and need to build resilience and self-reliance. Billionaires like Dangote and Nilekani are helping but many, many more of their peers need to join their ranks. Otherwise, the emerged world's demographic dividend may well turn into a curse, an issue which we turn to in the next chapter.

Notes

1 Africa's Richest Man and his $20 billion refinery –*The Wall Street Journal*, February 20, 2025.
2 Aliko Dangote: The Business Titan Transforming Africa's Economy –*CEO Today*, December 11, 2024.
3 Democracy in Nigeria – Explainer by Leena Koni Hoffman and Jon Wallace, Chatham House, June 29, 2022.

4 Nigeria's path to prosperity: From import dependence to export-led growth, Business Day, Nigeria, May 8, 2025.
5 The country's currency is the naira.
6 Resource curse exacerbates poverty in Nigeria – The Borgen Project, August 23, 2022.
7 What's the key to business success in Africa – Alvin Powell, Harvard, November 5, 2015.
8 Dangote Cement – An African Success Story – Africa Studies Centre, Leiden, the Netherlands, 2016.
9 Strategic Analysis of Dangote Cement –*DiamondBridge Economics and Business Journal* – Volume 3, Issue 2, April 2023.
10 China's Huaxin Cement to challenge Dangote, BUA after Lafarge Africa purchase –*The Africa Report*, December 9, 2024.
11 Solving Cement's Massive Carbon Problem –*Scientific American*, February 1, 2023.
12 The Notorious ESG – published by Emerald (UK), September 2023.
13 Full disclosure – I serve as an advisor to Gateway Partners, which holds a small stake in Dangote Cement. However, this chapter is based entirely on external sources and research.
14 Cement industry generates 7% of global emissions –*Construction & Engineering Digest*, November 27, 2023.
15 Is Aliko Dangote emulating Ambani in trying to turn Nigeria's oil curse into a blessing – Amit Jain, CNBC Africa, March 14, 2022.
16 Al Jazeera – In Nigeria's crude capital, a plan to win the war against oil theft – December 19, 2024.
17 BBC News report on the conference where Aliko Dangote spoke – Who wins when Nigeria's richest man takes on the "oil mafia" – November, 2024.
18 Africa's Richest Man Doubled His Fortune on A Massive – And Risky $23 billion Bet – Forbes Africa, February 17, 2025.
19 Reich is a former US Labour Secretary and has written extensively about what he describes as corporate capture of American politics. He is the author of *Supercapitalism – The Battle for Democracy in an Age of Big Business* (2008) and *Saving Capitalism* (2016).
20 The $200 Billion Gamble: Bill Gates's Plan to Wind Down His Foundation – *New York Times*, May 8, 2025.

Section III

The Fault Lines

Chapter 9

Youth

The emerged world has a surplus of restive youth at a time when the west is shutting its doors and AI could destroy jobs.

The phrase melting pot has come to symbolise America's long-standing open door policy towards immigrants and in step with the country's remarkable ability to absorb people from different cultures, ethnicities, beliefs, and blend them into a cohesive whole. The idea of America as a "beacon" and "shining city on the hill" is being increasingly challenged in recent years due to the rise of Trump and his peculiar brand of populist nationalism. While an overwhelming majority of Americans support legal immigration, if opinion polls are any indicator, there is a thin line dividing acceptance (of legal immigrants) and rejection (of illegals). This has created a virulent brand of populism which has tainted public discourse and undermined America's promise and potential for millions of immigrants wishing to study, work, and set up a life in the country. As a global macro trend, America's seeming rejection of immigration, which was one of the country's enduring organising principles, is having sharp reverberations all over the world. After all, where can youth in demographically rich countries like India, Indonesia, and sub-Saharan African turn to if the role model nation, America, shuts its doors and is increasingly becoming more hostile to the idea of accepting the world's "tired, your poor, your huddled masses yearning to be free".[1]The answer, in the short term at least, is Dubai and the United Arab Emirates (UAE).

I have been spending time in the Dubai and the UAE since the pandemic, partly as a solution to escape the East Coast of America's bone-chilling winters. The most remarkable aspect about living in Dubai is *how global* the emirate has become, a true melting pot of different nationalities and races. Superficially, this is evident in the coffee shop which I frequent each morning at the Dubai International Financial Centre (DIFC). The barista who greets me cheerfully is from Uganda and other staff includes two

DOI: 10.4324/9781003603375-13

Filipinos and an Indian. At DIFC's posher restaurants, the nationalities of the staff are also wildly diverse. I have encountered wait staff and managers who happen to be Colombian, Peruvian, Hungarian, Ukrainian, South African, and a dizzying cocktail of other nationalities.

To be sure, this is not an anomaly restricted to the DIFC. With the native population of the UAE limited to around 1.1 million, the emirate's overall population of 11 million is primarily foreign. If the UAE were the UK, population 70 million, this would be the equivalent of having an additional foreign-born population of 700 million. I exaggerate of course as the UK's foreign-born population as of 2025 was only around 10 million or around 17% of the total population of the country. There is fierce opposition even to this modest percentage, led by that country's politicians like Nigel Farage (with some public support), to roll back the country's liberal immigration policies. A similar phenomenon is unfolding across much of Europe, where countries are struggling to assimilate the new wave of arrivals, many of whom happen to be refugees fleeing persecution and violence in Syria, sub-Saharan Africa (SSA), and other unstable corners of the world. And America, where the foreign-born population soared to a record 53 million in 2024 or around 16% of the total population,[2] this surge has led to a fierce political backlash.

The rich world is not seeking to curb illegal and legal immigration alone. For a young person with resources anywhere in the world, tourism has been the most dependable way to expand horizons. A visit to the Louvre in Paris or the Vatican in Rome provides a first-time young visitor with a sense of world history and the sweep of civilisations and culture. Well, best of luck for anyone from the emerged world attempting to secure a tourist visa to travel to Europe, Canada, or America. The waiting time is inexplicable – applicants are given random waiting times for an interview, 420 days for a Canadian tourist visa in the case of a friend. Although Canadian or European authorities are likely to cite administrative reasons for the processing delays, the implicit message to the rest of the world cannot be simpler – don't bother to visit. If sustained over time, this will prove to be a real barrier and shrink global understanding, amity between young people in the emerged world and their rich counterparts.

The profound geopolitical question for the next decade is while the rich world may well succeed in tamping the flow of goods and services, in a rebuke to globalisation, can they afford to do the same with the flow of people? It is easy to place tariff and non-tariff barriers to restrict the flow of trade. But as America and any number of European countries will attest, it is near impossible to stem the flow of people, many of them illegal, who attempt in the millions to move to the high-income Western nations in search of a better life. The most visible manifestation of this is in demographics – the rich world, including China, Singapore, and Korea, are ageing rapidly while large countries and entire continents (India, Indonesia, SSA) have a surplus of youth.

The youth data on India and SSA are mind boggling. With 1.4 billion people, India is the world's most populous nation. Even the broad brush of the demographic data is startling – at least half of the country's population i.e. around 700 million is estimated to be under the age of 25. Two-thirds are less than 35. In theory, this gives India the bragging rights to have the world's largest workforce by 2027,[3] with an estimated billion people aged between 15 and 64. Anyone who has visited India can attest to the country's dramatic youth bulge. If you are above 50, you are likely to feel old in any public or private setting in India today. This has an impact, both positive and negative, in terms of the youthful energy on display in the country's urban centres, and negative, given the sheer volume of quality jobs which the government and private sector need to create to absorb the estimated 60 million people entering the employment market each year. India's economy is booming, with the government bragging that it is the fastest growing large economy in the G20, but even growth on steroids has limitations in terms of job creation.

As I wrote in a research paper for the Hinrich Foundation in 2024,[4] rising unemployment remains a major public concern and policy priority. Unemployment remains a major worry in the middle class and was a pivotal campaign issue in the 2024 general elections which dealt Modi a far narrower margin of victory than projected. "Government alone cannot possibly create the jobs required to absorb the millions entering into the workforce every year", said Rajeswari Sengupta, an associate professor from the Indira Gandhi Institute of Development Research in Mumbai. Youth unemployment rates have soared with data from the Centre for Monitoring Indian Economy (CMIE) showing that in the 12 months ended March 2023, unemployment in India's youth aged 20 to 24 years rose to 45%. Government data for the same period are significantly lower at 10%. "There is a mismatch between demand and supply of jobs, and it is becoming larger social issue in India", says Suyash Rai, deputy director and a fellow at Carnegie India. The government's former Chief Economic Advisor Kaushik Basu warned that India's youth unemployment rate was amongst the highest in the world. "This is doing deep damage", Basu said. "For the sake of the country, we must not hide behind slogans, must put politics aside and take corrective measures".

These problems are compounded in SSA, which as a whole is poorer than India but is facing a youth bulge of historic proportions. As the Population Reference Bureau noted in a paper,[5] by 2030, young Africans are expected to make up 42% of the world's youth and account for 75% of those under the age of 35 in Africa.

> With such a large population of young people, supportive policies and programs on inclusive youth development are critical now more than ever. Harnessing the demographic dividend and expanding opportunities for young people – to the benefit of all Africans – will require sound data and evidence on the status of African youth.

The World Bank estimates[6] that by 2075, one-third of the world's population – and of the working age population – will be African. It is the "only region" where the workforce will grow continuously in the coming decades. "Young people on the continent have aspirations, energy, and ambition. This is the most connected generation of Africans in history, one that can turn the trajectory of the continent", the World Bank report said. The growing working-age population presents an "enormous opportunity" to supercharge economic growth and lead to greater prosperity for billions of people on the continent. While the World Bank report is high on rhetoric, it ignores the practical realities of being a young person on the African continent. There are modest exceptions, Botswana and Rwanda come to mind, but it is no exaggeration to say that much of the continent is still mired in low economic growth, high debt, civil strife, and limited economic opportunity. We examined the dysfunction in Nigeria in a previous chapter, and an even more acute problem is that young people across the continent are ruled by a group of old men, with little sense of what their hopes and aspirations are. With limited prospects for advancement, it is inevitable that young Africans (and young people elsewhere) are voting with their feet and seeking opportunities elsewhere.

However, if you are a qualified Ghanaian dentist aspiring to move to the UK or America to study or work, your options at the moment are extremely limited. With America and Europe also making it more difficult to access avenues for legal migration, prospects elsewhere are also limited. In developed Asia, Singapore has also imposed restrictions for work visas, while pathways to Japan and Korea are even more difficult because of cultural barriers. China is host to a vast foreign student population, estimated at 500,000, but a majority of them return home after studies. In short, the dentist from Ghana would be tempted to move to the UAE instead, where he or she can secure a study or work visa literally on demand and face a more congenial and diverse work environment where almost all of your peers are foreign-born. Ironically, it is not only youth from the emerged world who have made a beeline to Dubai and the UAE in recent years. Escaping taxes and limited opportunities, the emirate has become a haven for thousands of young Europeans. At Taormina in Sicily, I encountered a young waiter who told me that he had aspirations of moving to Dubai to work for a high-end restaurant because he faced stagnant wages at home and even more limited prospects for upward mobility.

Writing for *Forbes,* Lissele Pratt writes that over the past five years, Dubai has proved itself as one of the "most stable investment hubs" in the world – particularly during the Covid-19 pandemic where other cities struggled to keep their heads above water. She notes that while financial business leaders are attracted to Dubai by financial incentives, it would be "naïve" to say that economics is the only factor at play here. This is because in order to attract the biggest investors in the world, you must also make your city an attractive place to live for that demographic. "Over the last two decades, I believe that Dubai absolutely achieved this, offering elite schools, world-class dining, top-tier healthcare and more affordable luxury housing than even cities like London", she writes[7] "Its strategic location (linking Switzerland and Singapore while anchoring the MENA region) helps make it a natural financial crossroads".

In short-order, Dubai has emerged as the Venice of our times and arguably as one of the world's last bastions of globalisation, as defined as the free movement of goods, services, capital, and people. What I find particularly intriguing about Dubai and its fellow emirates, the richest being Abu Dhabi, is that a significant proportion of the world's youth in the emerged world consider it as a model nation to aspire and move to. This is indeed a shock to more developed cities like New York or London who regard themselves as thriving, model epicentres for commerce, culture, and diversity. And I have data to support my proposition. Here are findings from the 2022 Arab Youth Survey commissioned by global PR firm Burson. For the 11th straight year, youth respondents in the 18–24 age group from the Arab world voted in overwhelming majorities (57%) in identifying the UAE as their top choice to live and work in, ahead of America (24%), Canada (20%), France (15%), and Germany (15%).

The research findings identified five factors for the UAE's continued attractiveness: its growing economy, its safe and secure environment, its generous salary packages, and the wide range of work opportunities it provides. The UAE also scored highly amongst this demographic as the country they hoped their own nation could model itself on. My friend Sunil John,[8] who used to run the Middle East operations of Burson and was the originator of the survey, told local media[9] that the UAE continued to be a "beacon of hope and opportunity", phrases usually associated with America, for young Arab men and women across the Middle East and North Africa.

> What is perhaps most telling is the fact that the UAE scores highly on all the issues that Arab youth said were most important to them in our research, such as job opportunities, education quality, and the preservation of the region's cultural traditions and values.

For Western readers, the emergence of Dubai as a "beacon of hope and opportunity" is likely to come as a shock. This is because Dubai is usually associated with other, more provocative labels – bling town, wild beach parties, playground for billionaires, and garish displays of wealth. These characterisations are not necessarily untrue but they provide a one-sided and misleading picture about why a significant section of the emerged world's youth view the emirate as a role model. This chapter of course is not only to extol the virtues of the UAE but to make the broader point about the emerged world becoming more confident and its young population not necessarily looking at America or Europe as a model. In their anti-immigrant rhetoric and specific policies to curb the inflows of immigrants, these nations are also making it clear that they no longer support one of the most cherished tenets of globalisation – the free movement of people, alongside deep ambivalence about the merits of free trade and investment.

Western sceptics are likely to raise several objections to my characterisation as America or Europe being comprehensively opposed to immigration and closed borders. It is difficult to deny the fact that voters by a significant margin have turned ambivalent about the merits of immigration. However, I accept their viewpoint and being an immigrant myself to the UK and America, to acknowledge that alarmist headlines in newspapers about the perils of immigration often mask the more positive fact that these nations have been fundamentally and positively transformed as a result of inflows of talent. It is hard to conceive of another nation besides America where the CEOs of the country's top tech firms – Alphabet, IBM, Microsoft, Adobe, Palo Alto Networks, and many, many more – are headed by Indian-origin Americans. This cohort is matched by migrant talent from Greater China – Jensen Huang of Nvidia, Lisa Su of AMD, and China's artificial intelligence (AI) architect Kai-fu Lee, who spent his formative years working for Microsoft in America. While China has resolutely shut its doors to cryptocurrencies, many crypto bros from the mainland have found America to be a lucrative hunting ground for business. This free flow of people has nurtured America's rise as a tech superpower, and it is arguable if constraining the flow of talent will see the creation of more home-grown founders and CEOs.

Think tank Centre for a New American Century (CNAS) is quite emphatic[10] about "three hard truths" when it comes to America's ability to hold on to technological supremacy vis-à-vis an ascendant China. First, America lacks the STEM workforce needed to unleash our tech potential. The country faces an estimated shortage of 1.4 million technicians, computer scientists, and engineers by 2030, and 90% of technology leaders say recruiting is a "major or moderate challenge". The second challenge identified by CNAS was the fact that America's tech pipeline "cannot" fill talent gaps in the short term. Expanding domestic STEM talent takes years, even decades. "One study found that the United States will require 300,000 more engineers than US universities will graduate by 2030 to realise the full potential of the CHIPS and Science Act". The final point, and perhaps the most sobering, that comprehensive immigration reform in America is "highly unlikely" anytime soon. "As technologies like AI advance at breakneck speed, holding a high-tech immigration fix hostage to a decades-long political stalemate risks irreversible damage to America's tech edge, and by extension our national security", the CNAS researchers concluded.

The skill shortages became evident when Taiwan Semiconductor (TSMC) unveiled plans to build a giant fab facility in Arizona in 2023 and 2024. Building a fab facility is not simply a task of constructing a giant factory – TSMC was looking for people with precision technical skills (engineers) as well as welders, fitters, electricians, and plumbers to get the facility off the ground. The Taiwanese company soon realised that it was difficult to source home-grown talent in these areas and started shipping technicians from Taipei to facilitate the process. This created a predictable political backlash in America because the primary objectives of federal government subsidies for the project were to reshore manufacturing to America and to create local jobs. This became even more controversial when US immigration raided a Hyundai EV battery plant under construction in Georgia in September 2025, detaining over 470 Korean workers on allegations of working illegally in the country. So, rich nations face a fundamental choice as they attempt to reconfigure the global economy after several decades of globalisation, which led to the rise of the emerged world, notably China.

While I have focused extensively on American ambivalence towards immigration, the same, if not more, can be said about peer nations in the rich world – Europe, Canada, Australia, Japan, Korea, and to a more limited extent New Zealand and Singapore. I concede that immigration is a privilege and sovereign states have the right to increase or limit people flows based on their special needs. Canada and Australia, two nations with roughly approximate populations, have been promiscuous in inviting newcomers over the past two decades. Since 2000, official estimates suggest that Canada approved permanent resident applications to the tune of roughly 250,000 a year[11] (which touched a peak of 464,000 in 2024). However, these flows are likely to slow in the decade ahead as Canada faces challenges in absorbing the new immigrants and creating job opportunities for them. Similarly, the Australian Bureau of Statistics estimates[12] that the country welcomed around 3 million legal migrants since 2000. The top source of these immigrants was India, which alone contributed to 500,000 of the new arrivals, no doubt driven by the intense competition for jobs at home. On the other hand, Japan and Korea, two rich East Asian nations with rapidly ageing populations, have also been shedding their hesitation to welcome new migrants, although not on the scale of Australia or Canada. Having spent a lot of time on work in these two countries, it is obvious that cultural barriers are significant for a newcomer to navigate.

If one had to build a hard-nosed business case for continued immigration benevolence by rich nations, it will be as follows. First, the emerged world has a surplus of youth seeking economic opportunity, education, and advancement. Second, these opportunities are limited at home because of the population bulge and failure of some governments to create jobs at home. Third, the rich world in contrast is ageing rapidly, America included. By the current trajectory, America and Europe will follow Japan by having a significant proportion of old people by 2050. The developed world needs access to a pool of skilled and unskilled labour. Finally, climate disasters in many parts of the emerged world – South Asia and Africa prominently, which we will discuss in the next chapter – are forcing mass migration, initially to the emerged country's urban centres and eventually across borders. If left unchecked, these climate refugees will swamp the rich world's ability to police illegal migration which is happening across land borders and on sea.

My thesis above will be regarded as naïve and with some disdain in many parts of the developed world. This is because the world has changed immeasurably since Donald Trump descended the Trump Towers escalator on June 16, 2015, to launch his candidacy for President. "A country without borders is, quite simply, not a country", he said,[13] promising to build a "massive wall" to secure America's southern border "Mexico is not our friend. They are beating us at the border and hurting us badly at economic development. They are sending people that they don't want – the United States is becoming a dumping ground for the world". Since Trump has been re-elected to office in 2024, his administration has doubled down on restricting immigration, allocating a massive $80 billion for the department responsible for deporting illegal immigrants. Trump has also waged war against America's storied institutions of higher learning like Harvard and has ordered tougher screening for foreign students wishing to study in the US. Although articulated in a different context, the Trump administration clearly wishes to build a "tall fence with a small yard"[14] around the country and return America to its early 20th-century isolationist roots.

There is a reasonable counter argument to put forward that rich countries are not responsible for absorbing surplus labour from the emerged world. This argument, however, would have resonated better during the globalisation era, which unofficially ended the moment Trump launched his candidacy. During that era, which stretched from the 1960s before sputtering in 2015, there was a global compact in place which allocated responsibilities for the rich and emerged world. I am simplifying of course but the compact ran somewhat along these lines. Wages were rising significantly in America and Europe, particularly in light manufacturing sectors like shoes, clothes, and toys. Multinational firms and distributors found it much more economical to produce this stuff in the emerged world – starting with Korea, Hongkong, Singapore, and Taiwan in the 1960s and extending to China and Southeast Asia in subsequent decades. The compact was balanced and not one-sided. The rich world benefited from a cost-effective and reliable supply chain for stuff which Western consumers could not do without. At the same time, East Asian countries benefited from rising investment in light manufacturing, creating quality jobs and allowing the workforce to absorb technical skills in manufacturing. It is difficult to find hard data on whether the rise of the East Asian tigers in the 1960s led to appreciable declines in emigration. In Singapore, where I have lived and worked for a decade, it is remarkable that an overwhelming majority of Singaporeans still prefer to return home after a stint abroad – either for study or work.

However, there is a sadder story to report from the economic front-lines of America and Europe. As the countries receiving these investments prospered, so should have the rich world because, in theory, the loss of jobs due to the exodus of light manufacturing should have been replaced with investments in more advanced sectors, with significant investments in work-force development and skills training. The tragedy of America's rust-belt is that while the state encouraged unfettered globalisation during the go-go 1990s – with the signing of free trade agreements like NAFTA – very little attention was paid to the left behind in Ohio, Kentucky, Pennsylvania and a vast swathe of America's manufacturing belt.

Economist Larry Summers, who served as Treasury Secretary under President Clinton when NAFTA was negotiated, has said that[15] the free trade agreement was a "watershed" as to whether America was going to stand for larger markets. He also expounds on the benefits to Mexico from the free trade agreement.

> I think it resulted in a profound change in the internal political dynamics in Mexico in favour of the progressive forces that believed in the market and friendship with the United States as opposed to forces that believed more in socialism and opposition to the United States.

Summers' name is also closely associated with the Clinton administration's decision in 2001 to allow for China's accession into the World Trade Organisation (WTO), which in the eyes of many economists and politicians in America essentially turbocharged the deindustrialisation of America and the rise of China as a manufacturing and economic powerhouse. It is no surprise that during China's boom years – which was launched in 1979 and lasted through at least 2016 – the country's young population was never more globalised and accessed educational opportunities at American and European elite institutions. However, a majority of them returned home because of the excess of opportunity.

The compact which I described between rich and emerged nations has frayed in the two and a half decades since China entered the WTO. There is a deep sense of betrayal and anger in America's once dominant manufacturing belt about successive lost generations due to lack of jobs and economic opportunity. It is no coincidence that these rust-belt states have also seen the highest rates of opioid abuse and deaths. There is strong evidence that automation played an equally important role in the loss of manufacturing jobs but politicians find it much easier to blame the "other", in this case China, rather than machines for the devastation.

While much of the responsibility and policy response to economic dislocation lies with American politicians and voters, there is an urgent need for new global compact because an even greater dislocation in jobs for youth is just around the corner – through the rise of AI. Sam Altman, the founder of OpenAI, has been forthright in his articulation of the impact of AI on jobs and society. He said that previous technological revolutions have also resulted in job displacements but "what's different about AI" is how quickly the disruption could be happening. "Over some period of time, society can adapt to a huge amount of job change and you can look at the last couple of centuries and see how much that's happened", he said,[16] adding that AI was compressing the speed of change "I don't think anyone knows exactly how fast this is going to go. But I feel like it could be pretty fast".

Let me paint a picture of what would happen to youth populations in the emerged world (and the world at large) should there be massive job losses due to the rise of AI. In two of the world's top ten economies – China and India – university graduates are finding it difficult to access job opportunities. I already illustrated India's challenges earlier in the chapter and China's is equally acute. The generation born in the late 1990s and 2000s is prepared to stay at home rather than slog long hours at public or private enterprises. Momentarily, this phenomenon was labelled the lying flat moment, or *tang ping*, because of the typical young graduate's aversion to the country's intense work culture. As the Brookings Institution put it,[17] China's drive towards technological independence has raised alarm bells in the West, where a resurgent China is widely considered the key strategic challenge of the 21st century. "But these fears all too often fail to consider the internal obstacles facing Beijing's push toward tech supremacy. Among them is one very low-tech problem: a prevailing sense of social and professional stagnation".

This sense of stagnation is likely to accelerate, in China and elsewhere, *if* the fears about AI decimating entire employable sectors materialise. There is a lot of hype on AI's promise and potential, for example, to replicate white-collar and blue-collar tasks and replace the vast segment of the work-force. I agree that policymakers should prepare for worse case scenarios and this should be a galvanising moment for the world. The IMF has warned[18] that "almost 40 percent of global employment" is exposed to AI. There are sharp variations depending on income levels. Historically, the IMF notes that automation and information technology have tended to affect routine tasks, "but one of the things that sets AI apart" is its ability to impact high-skilled jobs. Say goodbye then to lawyers, financial analysts, coders, journalists, and even authors like me. While emerged nations, according to the IMF study, face a lower impact from job losses compared with richer countries, the pinch point could be worse.

> These findings suggest emerging market and developing economies face fewer immediate disruptions from AI. At the same time, many of these countries don't have the infrastructure or skilled workforces to harness the benefits of AI, raising the risk that over time the technology could worsen inequality among nations.

What the IMF report under-states is the huge risks to social stability if young people in the emerged world, significantly in larger numbers compared with its rich counterparts, fail to find decent jobs and secure upward mobility, just as their parents did. There will be mutinies at home and a surge in illegal immigration. This is already unfolding through the so-called "Gen Z" protests in 2024 and 2025 in a diverse group of emerged and developing nations – Sri Lanka, Bangladesh, Nepal, Indonesia, and Morocco to name a few. The hard-won success of emerged nations in recent decades could potentially be wiped out *if* the AI wave negatively impacts the way we work and the way we live. What are the prospects then for greater global cooperation or coordination to intermediate on jobs and other pressing challenges? We turn to this contentious topic in the final chapter.

Notes

1 From the inscription on the Statue of Liberty, an 1883 sonnet by the poet Emma Lazarus.
2 All the population data have been gleaned from publicly available databases.
3 I have drawn data from multiple public sources including an article in India's MINT newspaper, September 8, 2017.
4 Roadblocks to India's manufacturing renaissance – research paper for the Hinrich Foundation, September 2024.
5 Africa's Future: Youth and the Data Defining Lives – Population Reference Bureau.
6 Investing in youth, transforming Africa – World Bank Group, June 27, 2023.
7 Investing Smartly As Dubai Aims for Global Financial Hub – Lissele Pratt, *Forbes*, May 8, 2025.
8 Full disclosure. I served as Senior Advisor of Burson in Dubai in 2022 and 2023 but was not involved in the survey.
9 A record two-thirds of young Arabs name the UAE as the country they would most like to live in – Zawya, September 21, 2022.
10 To Win The Tech Race, America Needs High-Skilled Immigration Reform – CNAS, December 4, 2023.
11 Data from public sources.
12 Australian Bureau of Statistics – Permanent migrants in Australia, March 29, 2023.

13 Speech by Donald Trump, Announcement of Candidacy – New York, June 16, 2015.
14 President Biden's national security advisor Jake Sullivan had used this phrase to describe America's industrial strategy and in limiting.
15 Larry Summers, interview with PBS – April 24, 2001.
16 Sam Altman testimony before US Senate Committee on Commerce, Science, and Transportation – May 8, 2025.
17 Brookings commentary – The "lying flat" movement is standing in the way of China's innovation drive, July 8, 2021.
18 AI will transform the global economy. Let's make sure it benefits humanity – IMF, January 14, 2024.

Chapter 10

Coexistence

The future of the world order hinges on a word cloud of Cs, starting with coexistence....with a dash of The Ten Commandments and threat of zombie fungi.

The English language has a surplus of words starting with the letter C, at least when it comes to discussing the world order. There are cooperation, collaboration, and coordination, essential for maintaining global economic stability. Cooperation works to prevent conflict, of which we've had a surfeit in recent years. Let's not forget the convening power of large nations like America and China, plus multilateral agencies like the UN. Coexistence is also a sound organising principle, built on principles when the world order was still nascent. For the other defining challenge of our era, climate, the world surely needs plenty of the above c's. In the absence of this, the multilateral system will surely fracture and the emerged world needs to build its own capacity to cope with and address the challenges, solely or in concert with peer powers. For emerged nations, who are on the cusp of assuming greater power and responsibilities, it is unfortunate that their role is being recognised just at a time when the world fragments.

Now, that I have concentrated minds on this issue, I would like to pivot to the letter e and discuss equality in the world order. As this book has hopefully advocated, the current world order is terribly unequal and the rules are terribly skewed in favour of the status quo powers. This is because the exercise and projection of world power is still based on the principle that might is right. The country with the largest navy, like Britain did starting with the 17th century, ruled the waves of Britannia and beyond. Spanish power in Latin America was built on the principle that the enormous wealth on the continent was simply there for the taking. More recently, the exercise of American power in the modern era has not only involved the implied threat of force (through the world's largest and most effective defence force) but also through economic means due to the dominance of the dollar. Crudely put, the post-World War II era not only ushered in a

DOI: 10.4324/9781003603375-14

period of unprecedented economic prosperity but also entrenched 19th century thinking about power and projection.

There is a deep-rooted, almost cynical belief that "mere good intentions", as former US diplomat Dennis Ross put it in a book review,[1] cannot prevail in the "anarchic" world of international affairs. "To prevent war, one must be prepared to wage it. Moral imperatives cannot guide policy because they tend to lead sooner or later to excesses, to absolutes. International law won't end conflicts or preclude them or even provide limits". This belief, in the essential nature of power which originated in 19th-century Europe, has permeated international relations ever since. Or as President George W. Bush memorably put it in his State of the Union address in January 2002, "You are either for us or against us". While large, powerful nations through millennia have always stood on the side of might, I would argue that today's world order calls for a differentiated, more collaborative approach. Japan's Defence Ministry has it exactly right when it said in its 2025 review[2] that the international community is now facing its greatest trial since the end of World War II. "The existing order of world peace is being seriously challenged, and Japan finds itself in the most severe and complex security environment of the post-war era".

To illustrate that a better collaborative way is possible, albeit on a minor scale, let me take you to the International Monetary Fund (IMF) in July 1998, when I joined as a press officer at the height of the Asian financial crisis. The first thing that struck me was the vast power differential which existed between "creditor" nations i.e. the G7, which supplied most of the usable capital for the fund, and "debtor nations" i.e. developing countries such as mine at the time (India) which borrowed from the IMF and relied on the munificence of powerful creditors. While the IMF is the crown jewel amongst multilateral institutions and still attracts the best economic talent, there were inequities for staff from developing countries which was impossible to overlook. One stark example was in the fund's formidable policy development and review department (PDR for short) whose senior ranks were always filled by nationals from the G7, with America and the UK dominating. PDR set the broad economic policies for the Fund, including the specific conditions under which borrower countries such as India accessed IMF loans to deal with crisis. While this was never explicitly set out as such, there was a belief at the time that setting PDR policies could possibly never be trusted with capable economist staff from say, Jamaica or Ghana.

However, in my 18-year tenure, the IMF changed dramatically and its shareholding began to reflect the new economic realities which were just emerging at the time. China was elevated in 1999 to become the sixth largest shareholder, and India's participation in the institution's Financial Transactions Program (FTP), which brought together creditor nations providing a pool of usable currency reserves for the IMF, was the precise moment when the world's balance of economic power began to shift. This shift, and further changes to the shareholding structure in 2010, which provided emerged nations with even greater voting rights and say in the institution, was made possible by successive administrations in Washington D.C. who took a pragmatic and sensible approach in providing greater voice and representation for emerged nations. I must add that Europe, which stood to lose the most from the shift in votes, was reluctant to endorse the changes and had to be dragged in. And yes, the senior staff composition of PDR, today called the Strategy, Policy, and Review department (SPR or short), also changed and it has had a set of remarkably diverse heads of department ever since, from both emerged and developed regions.

At the time, technocrats at America's Treasury Department may have come across as cold-hearted policy wonks but they recognised that disorderly power shifts would jeopardise the multilateral nature of the IMF and even risk global economic stability. This was the era of live and let live, where America was willing to take the wider global economic good into consideration in supporting reforms. Where are all of these technocrats now, I wonder, as the world lurches from crisis to crisis and the contours of the carefully designed international financial architecture are in peril. When I reflect on that sadly bygone era, where it was possible to reconfigure global power shifts without too much fuss, what comes to mind is that the America was upholding the principles of equality, fairness, and justice. In global affairs, this might seem to be impossibly high ideals to live by.

Indeed, philosopher and Nobel Prize winning economist Amartya Sen, who has devoted his career to examining these issues, has written[3] about the many inequities in the theories and actual application of justice. "Indeed, the theory of justice, as formulated under the current dominant transcendental institutionalism, reduces many of the most relevant issues of justice into empty – even if acknowledged to be "well meaning" – rhetoric". He writes that when people across the world agitate to get *more* global justice, they are not clamouring for some kind of "minimal humanitarianism".

> Nor are they agitating for a "perfectly just" world society, but merely for the elimination of some outrageously unjust arrangements to enhance global justice, as Adam Smith, or Condorcet, or Mary Wollstonecraft did in their own time, and on which public agreements can be generated through public discussion, despite a continuing divergence of views on other matters.

I understand that traditional definitions of power, in global affairs or economics, dictate that there will always be rule-makers (the powerful) and rule-takers (the less powerful). If philosophical notions of what constitutes justice, as articulated by Sen and others, are not materially relevant for world politics, is there then at least a recognition that a rules-based system should entrench fair treatment into the equation? In a 2010 paper for the Brookings Institution, Hakan Altinay acknowledges [4]the conventional view that fairness does not matter in managing our global challenges – only power does. This view is persistent across the international system, including from the periphery which is the emerged world. "They argue that might makes right and this absolves those without formidable power of any responsibility for solving global problems or even articulating their potential contributions if something other than the law of the jungle were to prevail".

The net result in Altinay's view – the "hubris" of the powerful triggers irresponsibility among the not so powerful, which in turn is used by the cynics to argue the need for unadulterated power, given the "rampant irresponsibility" in the world at large. In the current geopolitical context, this essentially means that with America and China absorbed in strategic competition and great power politics, there would be even a greater temptation for the world at large to stand back and play a passive role. Indeed, this is already happening in the climate domain where inaction by the G7 has sent a signal to the world at large to delay their own plans. Altinay is emphatic that "fairness" in global governance does matter today and will matter more in the future.

> Yet it is evident today that power disparities are less severe today and are likely to be even less so in the near future. At the same time the level of global interdependence and the very nature of the imminent global problems we face have clear repercussions for the minimum constellation of alliances that is necessary to overcome these problems.

For me personally, Sen and Altinay's thinking on the idea and application of justice and fairness in global affairs, sweeping in scope and built on moral foundations, are precisely the guiding principles we should deploy in addressing the current global conjuncture. The realists will point out that the train has left the station i.e. any chances of a smooth transition have been lost because of the accelerating strategic competition between the US and China and the chain reaction it has set in terms of countries attempting to understand their own choices and implications. I am also cognisant that there is wide consensus in the American policy apparatus that it was a strategic mistake to allow China to accede to the WTO at the turn of the century and to a more limited extent endorse changes to the IMF's shareholding structure. America's strategic gift to China has resulted in, at least according to the DC consensus, a resurgent China which is challenging America's status as a superpower. Therefore, the consensus goes, China must no longer be provided with special privileges and access. The view from Beijing, of course, is radically different with China regarding American actions as blatant attempt to ringfence its power and as part of a long-standing Western mindset to curtail and contain the country's rise.

Since this is a book, I can afford to ignore the realists and the international relations scholars, only for a moment, and take you on an alternative journey instead where both outcomes are possible – there is a smooth power transition and both developed and emerged nations have a shared seat on the high table. To get there, one must pay attention to recent examples – positive as well as the contrarian alternative, a more dire future scenario where the global transition is disorderly and disruptive and threatens to endanger the world we live in.

Let's go back to our c's and explore some of the fundamental tenets of international relations, starting with cooperation and coordination. In September 2008, the collapse of Lehman Brothers set in motion a series of unintended and unanticipated consequences which led to the global financial crisis. I have discussed the root causes of the crisis in a previous chapter and will focus here on something more prosaic – a large, rectangular table inside the stately National Building Museum in Washington D.C., where President George W. Bush had invited heads of state from the world's top 20 nations in terms of economic weight for the November 2008 G20 summit. President Bush was a lame duck leader at the time, about to cede power to Barack Obama in a few months. The summit was held on a chilly Friday and Saturday and the mood was sombre. The global economy had gone into freefall a few months earlier and the epicentre of the crisis, unlike almost previous episodes of the three decades prior, was advanced nations, America and Europe. There was Manmohan Singh, India's Prime Minister, who was also a renowned crisis fighter in his own right, having shepherded the country during the dark days of 1991 when the country almost went bankrupt. Singh's sagely advice to world leaders on how to resolve the global crisis, particularly those from Europe and America, was a turning of the tables moment in recent economic history. The mentee was preaching to the mentor on the virtues of rebuilding investor confidence.

For someone who has witnessed economic crisis first-hand for much of my professional career it is hard to describe my mixed feelings at the time. The depth and scope of the crisis was downright scary. Many of America and Europe's storied financial institutions were teetering on the brink and had to be bailed out by the state. There were inevitable feelings of *schadenfreude* to see rich nation policymakers, who had preached from their own shaky pulpit to emerged nations for a long time, to feel the full impact of an economic crisis at home. Personal feelings aside, the important question then was how the international community would respond to the crisis. In my view, it responded remarkably well and in a short period of time to restore sentiment and build the foundations for economic recovery. The recovery process was never going to be easy, as Greece demonstrated, but there was a strong consensus within the G20 to show global solidarity and support.

The Washington D.C. G20 summit represented peak international cooperation and coordination, which was followed up by the equally successful April 2009 London summit. From literally out of nowhere, the G20 had emerged as the most important global economic platform to cooperate, coordinate, and *make decisions* on most urgent issues. In a show of support and an unthinkable development today, China announced that it was launching a $586 billion fiscal stimulus program, equivalent to an eye popping 13% of GDP, to stimulate domestic and global economic growth. To be sure, China has suffered serious economic indigestion from that stimulus program, leading to chronic industrial overcapacity, zombie firms, and spiralling debt. However, it stands out even today as a demonstration of international solidarity.

"The challenges we face as a community of nations today are increasingly those of collaboration and cooperation, fighting climate change, rebuilding the global financial system and promoting sustainable economic development", wrote then United Nations (UN) Secretary General Ban Ki Moon.[5] He was also achingly optimistic when he declared that the world stood "on the threshold of a new multilateralism" and the "pendulum of history" was swinging back towards the UN and collective action. Those were naïve and optimistic thoughts, written when the world appeared to be briefly working in concert to address the severe global economic impact from a once-in-a-generation crisis.

Let's now turn to another recent example where the international community stumbled in coordination and cooperation on a global crisis – the coronavirus pandemic which shuttered the world in March 2020 and tragically claimed over 18 million lives. In contrast with the global financial crisis, the overall international response to Covid was slow, uncoordinated, and this cost lives. Now, there are substantial differences between dealing with a financial crisis and a pandemic. The latter was a global health emergency, and the virus spread invisibly through respiratory droplets and aerosols from infected individuals. While money was essential, as in a typical financial crisis, effectively addressing a global pandemic requires deep inter-country and intra-country coordination. It is evident that the international community at best merited a C rating (another C!) in its handling of the health emergency. Some countries were too early to lock down, many others too late, creating an imbalance in country responses. This also raised the risk of infection, and it was astonishing to see that in 2020, our modern era, rich countries struggled to deal with shortages of basic medical necessities like masks. However, not everything was negative with the Covid response as the world did considerably better in managing the development of the vaccine. Whatever President Trump's faults in 2020, his administration did a superb job in incentivising and coordinating the development of an effective vaccine in record time. Similar initiatives succeeded in Europe and further afield in India, which is a vaccine production superpower. There were inequities in the delivery of vaccines with many developing countries feeling they were on a long waiting list to receive supplies, which undoubtedly had humanitarian consequences. This is where countries like China and India stepped in by donating some of their own vaccine supplies to low-income nations in Asia, Africa, and Latin America.

When I look at the world today, I have serious doubts on whether the G20 will be as collegial and as effective as it was in 2008 and 2009 and if a future global pandemic response will even yield moderately positive results. How will the current or future G20 address this crisis? Will its leadership have the vision and focus, as its forbears demonstrated in 2008, or are we destined to journey down the slippery slope of uncertainty? This is a reasonable scenario to test out because the G20 has not been functioning as an effective global economic coordinating body of late. While the grouping does not have a permanent secretariat and host duties rotate each year, the entire exercise today resembles a global platform on mute mode. G20 officials burn thousands of air-miles in attending the approximately 50–60 meetings which are held year round, culminating in a leader's meeting. Solemn communiques are issued but it is difficult to discern if world leaders are actually moving the needle in resolving global economic issues. Indeed, as I write this America boycotted the 2025 G20 summit, hosted by South Africa, and appears to have barred thar nation from participating in the 2026 series of meetings, which it will host.

Let me sketch out a deliberately scary scenario to map out the likely international response in a future crisis. The scenario I have in mind is a blend of global economic crisis and a pandemic in 2050, a random year into the future, which originates in a group of developed and emerged nations. Global cooperation has frayed, the use of the dollar has fallen, and trade is restricted to three major economic blocs. Global GDP growth has stalled for several decades as the promise, potential, and indeed enthusiasm towards free trade and investment has waned. Since financial markets are no longer integrated, there are pockets of crisis all over the globe with no clear resolution pathways. China has relaxed capital controls over the renminbi, allowing an offshore market centred in Hongkong (which has shelved its currency's peg with the US dollar) to flourish once again. The euro is a serious challenger to the dollar, with the EU Commission's decision in 2030 to merge with the European Central Bank (ECB), and the euro bloc now encompasses 36 members, including new entrants the UK, Australia, New Zealand, Canada, and Ukraine. Over in America, the administration's decision in 2030 to start imposing a financial transactions tax on all US dollar-denominated transactions worldwide is initially a hugely successful effort in reducing the country's debt burden. However, the tax comes with costs as the rest of the world sharply minimises the use of the dollar in international transactions.

In 2050, our scenario year, the G20 and the multilateral system is in deep coma. A more assertive BICS grouping (the I stands for Indonesia), now with 140 members and excluding India and Russia, has become an important coordinating body for the emerged world, with renminbi as the de facto reserve currency. The expanded BICS, headquartered in Riyadh, has a permanent secretariat with joint leadership at the top (a Brazilian and South African serve as co-secretary general). It has its own monetary fund and development bank. The former G7 has splintered into two separate blocs – An American-dominated grouping called "Amerirus", which includes Russia, Hungary, Israel, Italy, and much of Latin America, excluding Brazil. And a bigger Trans-European and Pacific grouping, called Trans Eurasia, which includes the expanded EU, Asean (excluding Indonesia), India, Japan, and Korea. India and the UAE are the only countries with membership to both the BICS (where they have been relegated as observers) and Trans Eurasia but have preferred to peg their currencies to the Euro.

To war game this even further, imagine a fragmented world with three distinct trade, investment, and currency zones. The BICS bloc widely uses the renminbi, Trans Eurasia has mostly embraced the euro, and "Amerirus" the dollar. In theory, these distinct economic blocs should be water tight i.e. they trade and invest mostly with themselves and therefore minimise foreign currency risk, which bedevilled the former emerging world for several decades. Each of the economic zones has high tariff barriers for trade and investment. What could possibly go wrong?

The world's climate for a start. With the collapse of the UN-led multilateral climate negotiation process, climate change has accelerated with the world hurtling towards climate devastation on an unprecedented scale. Global temperatures have soared beyond 3.5 degrees above pre-industrial levels. All blocs are particularly vulnerable because they include many developing countries on the frontline of climate vulnerability. Global warming has also unleashed wave upon wave of deadly pandemics – originating from the uncontrolled expansion of the mosquito population and an unrelated and even more lethal toxin originating from cordyceps, a so-called zombie fungi which infects humans and soon manipulates their behaviours, turning them into a deadly fighting force. If the cordyceps scenario sounds familiar, hat tip to the video game and HBO streaming series, *The Last Of Us*,[6] from which this scenario has been shamelessly stolen.

To place things in historical perspective, the world has never faced a troika of menaces stemming from a global cordyceps and malaria pandemic, followed by economic devastation on a scale not even seen during the two World Wars. The three dominant blocs are soon reeling from an economic, public health, political, and social crises of unprecedented magnitude. The pandemic is also bloc agnostic i.e. it has equally impacted "Amerius", Trans Eurasia, and the BICS, claiming over 100 million lives globally. National governments are falling across the three economic blocs and an early casualty is social cohesion, as the zombie force controls major urban centres and challenges state authority. The uninfected have clustered around a few rural communities and have militarised, also diluting the authority of a centralised state. There is one ray of hope, however. Long before the world crumbled into three distinct economic blocs, the international community had collaborated on a joint response on a range of pandemic scenarios, including the uncontrolled expansion of the mosquito population and the risks from zombie fungi. An effective dual-shot vaccine could feasibly be developed with several stumbling blocks – "Amerius" possesses the historic scientific knowledge and innovation on pandemic research and containment through the CDC and National Institutes of Health. Trans Eurasia and the BICS excel in vaccine development. In order to rush to develop a vaccine, the three economic blocs have to shed their usual hostility towards each other and collaborate. A transnational group of scientific and public health experts are soon convened by the G3 to jointly develop the vaccine.

The G3 leadership of "Amerirus", Trans Eurasia, and the BICS, as it soon became known, also recognised that in the pre-existing historic world order, there existed a multilateral system of global agreements and cooperation which were established precisely to deal with the kind of crisis they were faced with. As restoring public health and containing the pandemic became over-riding priorities, the G3 soon decided that the only way out was to rebuild a system where cooperation, coordination, and collaboration were foundational guiding principles. By 2055, five years after the spread of zombie fungi, the G3 released the first batch of effective vaccines across the three economic blocs. It took another three years to restore control and vaccinate everyone because of the severe implosion in central authority and the inability of the state to deliver public goods.

In this eight-year period, the G3 leadership, in solidarity, agreed to dissolve their three economic blocs and scholars were drafted to help recreate a world order which existed before 2030. That order, soon called Earthsphere 3.0, placed multilateralism at the heart of how everything was going to be organised and the world, circa 2060, reestablished successor institutions to the UN, the World Bank, and the IMF. Instead of the G20 and G7 of yore, the G194 vowed to work cooperatively and through the multilateral system to deliver economic opportunity. With the rapid development of digital technologies, the world also had a new currency – the *Eartha* which replaced the dollar, the euro, and the renminbi as the world's *only* currency. There were important differences in global governance, circa 2060 compared with its predecessor. Every nation had a seat and equal voice on the table, which was a repudiation of how global power functioned in the pre-Earthsphere era. By pooling resources and talent, the international community pledged never to return to the new dark ages which existed between 2025 and 2050.

Now, I admit that I have either scared readers with the cordyceps scenario (all I can say is that you must see *The Last Of Us)* or perhaps even bored them because an implosion in the world order only exists in the realm of science fiction. My response – try to go back in time, perhaps to 1919, when the world was recovering from the horrors of World War I and soon faced the infamous Spanish influenza pandemic, which wiped out millions of people all over the world. Not surprising, because the world was as unprepared for the war which broke out in 1914 and there was no global governance to speak of even after the allies prevailed over Germany four years later.

When geopolitical experts talk loosely today about the inevitability of another world war, perhaps centred around China's invasion of Taiwan, I am reminded of World War I historian Christopher Clarke's sober warning, to put it mildly, about the far-reaching global impact of that conflict. "First, the war unleashed the demons of political disorder, extremism, and cruelty that disfigured the 20th century", he writes,[7]"It destroyed four multi-ethnic empires (the Russian, German, the Austro-Hungarian, and the Ottoman). It killed at least ten million young men and wounded at least twenty million more". He emphasised that the war "disorganised" the international system in immensely destructive ways. "Without this conflict it is difficult to imagine the October revolution of 1917, the rise of Stalinism, the ascendancy of Italian fascism, the Nazi seizure of power or the Holocaust". The war was, as Clarke reminds us, what historian Fritz Stern described as the "first calamity of the 20th century, the calamity from which all other calamities sprang".

My message therefore to those who believe in the inevitability of a future war between the US and China is a simple one – be careful what you wish for. I am not being a naïve and sentimental pacifist in calling for restraint and for the international community to double down on cooperation. The ultimate goal should be coexistence, a phrase which has disappeared from the geopolitical vocabulary for decades. It has controversial origins, in the former Soviet Union, and widely adopted by China in the 1950s in its relations with India. The phrase has fallen out of favour in the emerged world too, particularly after China violated the bilateral principle of peaceful coexistence and invaded India in the winter of 1962. In the 1960s, U Thant, the first Asian Secretary General of the UN was also a powerful advocate and defined coexistence on the simple principle that we are "thrown together" on this planet and "we have to live together".

"That is why the (UN) Charter imposes the imperative of all human beings to practice tolerance and to live together in peace with one another as good neighbours. To my mind this is the simplest definition of peaceful coexistence".[8]

In the current era, coexistence is not merely a pretty phrase but can be a sound organising principle on which the international community can reconfigure global governance. I call this **coexistent multilateralism,** CM for short, a new and improved rules-based international order (NRBIO) where the emerged world has equal voice and representation alongside the status quo powers. Rather than wait for a further deterioration in global cooperation, or indeed allow my extreme cordyceps scenario outlined above to materialise, the world must act now. To return to the Ten Commandments, coexistent multilateralism should have also a set of ten rules, conventions, dos, don'ts which should govern global affairs for the next few decades. It builds on the RBIO but removes the automaticity that the fate of all pressing global issues should be determined by hegemonic powers with the greatest defence force or economic might. CM's ten new commandments, delivered to the world from the heights of Mountain Earth, shalt be the following:

1 Global problems – economic crisis, pandemics, climate change – require global collaborative solutions.
2 Humans are a single planet species, and we commit to preserving and protecting Mother Earth.
3 In global governance, might is not right and all countries are recognised with equal voice and representation.
4 "This is not the era of war",[9] and the only conflicts worth waging are against poverty, climate, inequality, human rights violations, and other global scourges.
5 Countries which misbehave, either through mercantilist economic practices or through indulging in conflict, face the risks of sanctions and other tools of economic statecraft from the entire international community.
6 Artificial intelligence and new technologies are a threat to jobs and economic opportunity, which requires shared global solutions to support youth empowerment.
7 Countries have the autonomy and the agency to pursue independent economic policies as long as it does not clash with the global good.
8 A redefined multilateralism calls for nation-states to exercise greater power on global issues and for the scaling back of permanent multilateral bureaucracies.

9 The international community commits to equality and equity as an organising principle – cutting across global governance, gender, low-income countries and communities, and other disadvantaged groups.
10 Global debt and economic imbalances can jeopardise global stability, and countries commit to work cooperatively in building sustained, equitable, and balanced growth.

I have to explain Commandments 3 and 8 in some detail. On global governance, I am not calling for a recreation of the dysfunction which currently exists in the UN system, notably in the General Assembly, which is a powerless platform for the emerged world. A revamped global governance system, with a much higher vote share of the emerged world in global bodies such as the UN and the IMF, will address some of the shortcomings and weaknesses in the existing order and may even lead to better outcomes.

Similarly, on Commandment 8, as a former international civil servant, I can't believe I am calling for a scaling back in the permanent international bureaucracies which exist today in the multilateral system. There must be a better way to provide global public goods and the G20 and G7 process, which when it functioned well, serves as a good role model. The multilateral system should be preserved as an essential global platform but there is no reason why the UN system should employ over 37,000 staff in its secretariat, some of them dealing with issues which are better left for national governments to determine in concert with peer nations. Preserving the best of the rules-based order, strengthening global governance through a fair and equitable process, and with the ultimate goal of preventing conflict should be principles which every nation should have little difficulty in subscribing to. At the heart of what I am proposing is an idealistic new order, which just in time pulled the world back from the precipice of fragmentation and chaos. Getting there will require a lot of give and take, a belief in coexistence, in live and let live, and an enthusiastic commitment that our world is worth preserving and building on. The emerged world, the global economy's better half, deserves to play a prominent role in this renewed world order. Let's get to work.

Notes

1 Tragedy and Power – Dennis Ross, *Jewish Review of Books*, Fall 2020.
2 Defense of Japan – Annual White Paper, 2025. Ministry of Defense, Japan.
3 Sen's magisterial "The Idea of Justice" is essential reading for those who want to learn more about its foundational precepts (published in 2009, Allen Lane).
4 Hakan Altinary – Does Fairness Matter in Global Governance, Brookings Institution, October 2010.
5 Solidarity the solution to cascading crises – Ban Ki Moon, United Nations, December 2, 2008.

6 The Last of Us was a hugely popular video game before becoming an equally successful streaming series on HBO. It is a deeply moral story about a world in crisis and diminishing of trust in the world order.
7 From the *London Review of Books*, *The First Calamity*, by Christopher Clarke, August 29, 2013.
8 U Thant served as Secretary General between 1961–1971. The quote above is from a speech he delivered in January 1964.
9 The precise quote said to have been conveyed by Indian Prime Minister Modi to President Putin, following the Russian invasion of Ukraine.

Acknowledgements

If it takes a village to raise a child, it literally takes the world to bring a book of this kind across the finishing line. I am indebted to a great number of people for giving me the time to discuss the topics set out in the book and in challenging many of my early assumptions. I would like to start by thanking my publisher Routledge (Bethany Nelson and Meredith Norwich in particular) and to my agent Chris Newsom for his timely advice and for making this project happen. I have enjoyed conversations which feature in the book with several friends, mentors, and colleagues over the years. They include Sir David Manning and Sanjaya Baru, who generously endorsed the book. I would also like to thank the late Stanley Fischer, Vish Shankar, Sunil John, Josh Lipsky, Jeremy Mark, Salil Tripathi, Udaibir Das, Mahmood Pradhan, Sir Jeremy Greenstock, Nick Greenstock, Jack Lambert, Nathalie Wlodarcyk, Ambereen Choudhury, Andrew Bainbridge, Vikram Khanna, John Kang (my editor at *Forbes Asia*, where I write a monthly column), Taimur Baig, Nicholas Gordon, Kamar Jaffer, Khaldoun Hejaz, Yap Chuin Wei, Gary Litman, Alejandro Reyes, Rhodri Williams, Prakash Loungani, and Naresh Fernandes. The multiple movie references in the book are a tribute to my late friend Satyaprasad. I have also spoken with several policymakers in the emerged world, current and former, who prefer to remain anonymous.

This book is dedicated to the late Dion Fernandes, a mentor and beloved family member whose thinking and beliefs about scholarship, compassion, and humility were both of and ahead of his time. It is also dedicated to Hyderabad, my southern Indian hometown where I was raised and received a priceless education, not always through formal channels! As always, I would like to thank my wife Ferzine and daughter Neha for their steadfast love and support.

Vasuki Shastry
Washington D.C. and Dubai
December 2025

Index

Note: Page numbers followed by 'n' refer to notes.

For Product Safety Concerns and Information please contact our EU
representative GPSR@taylorandfrancis.com
Taylor & Francis Verlag GmbH, Kaufingerstraße 24, 80331 München, Germany

www.ingramcontent.com/pod-product-compliance
Ingram Content Group UK Ltd.
Pitfield, Milton Keynes, MK11 3LW, UK
UKHW022355190926
475702UK00015B/2302
* 9 7 8 1 0 3 2 9 9 2 9 7 6 *